WRITERS AND THE

ISOBEL ARMSTR
General Edit

D1646035

CGR
HPC

42C

Hampshire County Council

LIBRARY SERVICE

WINCHESTER REFERENCE LIBRARY
81 NORTH WALLS, WINCHESTER
Tel: 01962 846059
Fax: 01962 856615

For use in the

Library only

C003871652

CL.14.20k(11/97)

DIV.
Account

JOHN WILMOT, 2ND EARL OF ROCHESTER

a portrait by an unknown artist (1665-70), courtesy of the National Portrait Gallery, London

W

JOHN WILMOT, EARL OF ROCHESTER

GERMAINE GREER

Northcote House
in association with the
British Council

HAMPSHIRE COUNTY LIBRARY

R821
ROC

0746308884

C003871652

© Copyright 2000 by Germaine Greer.

First published in 2000 by Northcote House Publishers Ltd, Horndon House,
Horndon, Devon PL19 9NQ, United Kingdom.
Tel: +44 (01822) 810066 Fax: +44 (01822) 810034.

All rights reserved. No part of this work may be reproduced or stored in an
information retrieval system (other than short extracts for the purposes of review)
without the express permission of the Publishers given in writing.

British Library Cataloguing-in-Publication Data
A catalogue record for this book is available from the British Library

ISBN 0-7463-0888-4

Typeset by PDQ Typesetting, Newcastle-under-Lyme
Printed and bound in the United Kingdom

Contents

Biographical Outline

(A conscientious attempt has been made
to enter only dates that can be verified)

1647	1 Apr.	John Wilmot is born at Ditchley.
1652	13 Dec.	Poet's father created Earl of Rochester
		Attends grammar school in Burford.
1658	19 Feb.	Poet's father dies in Holland.
1660	18 Jan.	Entered as a Fellow Commoner at Wadham College, Oxford.
	May	'To His sacred Majesty'.
	Dec.	'Impia Blasphemi'.
1661	Jan.	'To her sacred Majesty the Queen Mother'.
	Feb.	Granted a pension of £500 p.a. by the King.
	9 Sept.	Awarded degree of M.A.
	21 Nov.	Begins European tour with Sir Alexander Balfour.
1662		Travelling in Europe.
1663		Travelling in Europe.
1664		Mother appointed Groom of the Stole to the Duchess of York.
		Mother seeks Elizabeth Malet as wife for her son; secures support of the King, Chancellor and Castlemaine.
	25 Dec.	Returns to England with letter for the King from his sister, the Duchess of Orleans.
1665	26 May	Attempts to marry Elizabeth Malet by capture. Is imprisoned in the Tower.
	19 June	Released from the Tower.
	6 July	Reports to Lord Sandwich to join Bergen expedition.
	12 Sept.	Sent by Sandwich with dispatch to the King.

	Makes the acquaintance of Henry Savile.
31 Oct.	Receives a gift of £750 from the King.
1666 21 Mar.	Appointed Gentleman of the Bedchamber.
31 May	Joins Sir Edward Spragge for sea-battle against the Dutch.
1 Oct.	At the calling of the House of Lords is listed as *infra ætatem*.
15 Nov.	Dances at Queen's Birthday Ball.
1667 29 Jan.	Marries Elizabeth Malet at Whitehall.
4 Feb.	Takes his wife to see *Heraclius* at the Duke's Playhouse.
June	Receives commission as Captain of Prince Rupert's Regiment of Horse Guards.
July	Summoned to House of Lords, though still a minor.
Oct.	Attends House of Lords on 11 days out of 14.
Nov.	Attends House of Lords on 12 days out of 21.
Dec.	Attends House of Lords on none of 16 days.
1668 17 Feb.	Attends House of Lords on 1 of 17 days.
28 Feb.	Warrant as gamekeeper for Co. Oxon.
Mar.	Attends House of Lords on 2 of 19 days.
Apr.	Attends House of Lords on 1 of 24 days.
14 Apr.	Petitions for grant of 4 bailiwicks in Wychwood Forest.
May	Attends House of Lords on 2 of 8 days.
Aug.	With Elizabeth.
late Nov.	His money and clothes stolen by a prostitute.
1669 16 Feb.	Dines at the Dutch embassy.
	Boxes Thomas Killigrew's ears.
17 Feb.	Is seen walking familiarly with the King.
	Is involved in a duel with Duke of Richmond and James Hamilton.
12 Mar.	Leaves for Paris.
12 Apr.	Writes to wife from Paris.
28 Apr.	Lady Anne Wilmot born.
6 May	At Adderbury.
	Returns to Paris.
Oct.	Attends House of Lords on 2 of 7 days.
Nov.	Attends House of Lords on 4 of 18 days.
23 Nov.	A duel is prevented between Rochester and the Earl of Mulgrave.

	Dec.	Attends House of Lords on 3 of 10 days.
1670	Feb.	Absent from all 6 sittings of House of Lords.
	Mar.	Absent from all 27 sittings of House of Lords.
	late Mar.	With Elizabeth at Adderbury.
	Apr.	Absent from all 8 sittings of House of Lords.
	June	In London, lodging in Portugal Row.
		Loses all his money at play, borrows £500.
	Oct.	Attends 1 of 3 sittings of House of Lords.
	Nov.	Attends House of Lords on 6 of 9 days.
	Dec.	Absent from all 18 sittings of House of Lords.
1671	2 Jan.	Lord Charles Wilmot christened.
	Jan.	Absent from all 21 sittings of House of Lords.
	Feb.	Absent from all 22 sittings of House of Lords.
	Mar.	Absent from all 24 sittings of House of Lords.
	Apr.	Attends House of Lords on 4 of 18 days.
	June	In Bath on his way to Somerset
	early Dec.	'Mistress Knight's Advice to the Duchess of Cleveland'.
	mid-Dec.	Quarrels at the playhouse with Richard Newport.
1672		Two poems published in *A Collection of Poems, Written upon Several Occasions, by Several Persons*.
	1 Feb.	At Adderbury for his half-niece's wedding.
	Feb.	In disgrace.
	Mar.	Pursuing £3,375 unpaid stipend.
	July	Travels into Somerset with wife and daughter.
	29 Aug.	Still at Enmore, Somerset.
	Sept.	Ill, pawns his plate to pay his doctor's fees. *Upon Nothing*.
1673	Feb.	Attends House of Lords on 5 of 13 days.
	Mar.	Attends House of Lords on 20 of 25 days before adjournment.
		A Ramble in St James's Park, circulating.
		Lampoon: 'Too long the wise Commons' circulating.
	21 Mar.	News of duel with Viscount Dunbar.
	22 Mar.	Bound over to keep the peace.
		Prologue to *The Empress of Morocco*.
	Apr.–May	Dryden writes to him at Adderbury.
	Oct.	Attends House of Lords on 3 of 4 days.
		With Elizabeth at Adderbury.

	Winter	'I' th' isle of Britain...'
		Letter from Mistress Price to Lord Chesterfield.
1674	Jan.	Absent from all 20 sittings of House of Lords.
	27 Feb.	Appointed Ranger of Woodstock Park.
		Attends House of Lords on 6 of 18 days before prorogation.
	13 July	Lady Elizabeth Wilmot christened.
		Artemisa to Cloe.
	Dec.	Acts as second for Savile in duel against Mulgrave.
	Winter	*A Satire against Mankind.*
		'A Pastoral Dialogue between Alexis and Strephon'.
1675	24 Feb.	Is denounced from the pulpit of Stillingfleet.
		Adds 50 lines to *A Satire against Mankind.*
	late Mar.	With Elizabeth at Adderbury.
	Apr.	Attends House of Lords on 5 of 13 days.
	30 Apr.	Sir Allen Apsley surrenders mastership of King's hawks to Rochester and William Chiffinch.
	May	Attends House of Lords on 9 of 20 days.
		Epilogue to *Love in the Dark* by Sir Francis Fane.
	June	Attends House of Lords on 5 of 8 days before prorogation.
	25 June	With friends smashes the King's glass chronometer.
	Aug.	Ill, in the country, has a fall from his horse.
	Sept.	Ill, in the country.
	Oct.	Attends House of Lords on 5 of 7 days.
	29 Oct.	Is unable to attend hearing about Rangership with Countess of Lindsey, sends proxy.
	Nov.	Absent from all 14 sittings of House of Lords.
		'An Allusion to Horace'.
		Adapts Fletcher's *Valentinian.*
		'Tunbridge Wells A Satire' published in *Proteus Redivivus.*
1676	6 Jan.	Lady Malet Wilmot christened.
	Feb.	In disgrace, rusticated, reported dead.
		Writes the farce *Sodom.*
	Apr.	*A New Collection of the Choicest Songs* licensed.
		'On the Supposed Author of a Late Poem in Defence of Satyr.'
	7 Apr.	Sir Robert Howard writes to him at Adderbury.

	17 June	Fracas at Epsom.
	2 Sept.	Dines with the Earl of Anglesey and Lucy Hutchinson.
1677	Feb.	Attends House of Lords on 4 of 9 days.
	Mar.	Attends House of Lords on 13 of 27 days.
	Apr.	Attends House of Lords on 5 of 13 days.
		Attends House of Lords on 1 of 5 days.
		Petitions for Buckingham's release from the Tower.
		Song: 'I swive as well as others do'.
		Epilogue to *Circe, a tragedy* by Charles Davenant.
		Songs for i 2 & 3 Voyces Composed by Henry Bowman.
	Aug.	At Woodstock.
	16 Dec.	Elizabeth Barry gives birth to the poet's daughter, Hester.
1678	15 Jan.	Attends House of Lords on 1 of 4 days.
	25 Feb.	Attends House of Lords on 1 of 20 days.
	Mar.	Absent from all 22 sittings of House of Lords.
	Apr.	Attends House of Lords on 1 of 5 days.
	13 Apr.	Petitions for lands in Ireland.
	May	Absent from all 16 sittings of House of Lords.
	June	Absent from all 21 sittings of House of Lords.
	Sept.	Quarrels with Lords Lovelace and Norreys at John Cary's house in Woodstock.
	Oct.	Absent from all 10 sittings of House of Lords.
	Nov.	Attends House of Lords on 11 of 25 days.
	Dec.	Attends House of Lords on 4 of 24 days.
1679	Winter	At High Lodge until February.
	Feb.	In London, in good health.
	Mar.	In House of Lords for the opening, takes the oath.
		Attends House of Lords on 16 of 20 days.
		My Lord All-Pride.
	Apr.	Attends House of Lords on 17 of 24 days.
	May	Attends House of Lords on 18 of 23 days before prorogation.
	Autumn	Falls ill.
	Oct.	'continues exseeding ill'.
1680	27 Jan.	Attends House of Lords.
	3 Feb.	At High Lodge, which is damaged by a great fire

	'made to air the house'.
Apr.	In London.
	Attempts to ride to Somerset, collapses, brought back in coach.
1 June	Thought to be dying, marvellously reformed.
15 June	Milch asses procured.
19 June	Signs remonstrance.
22 June	Adds codicil to will.
26 June	Dictates letter summoning Burnet.
20 July	Burnet arrives, poet has convulsion fit and raves.
24 July	Burnet leaves.
26 July	Dies.
9 Aug.	Is buried at Spelsbury.

Note

Readers will observe that this discussion uses three different sources for Rochester's text. For the poems I have used the edition by Keith Walker, *The Poems of John Wilmot, Earl of Rochester* (Oxford and New York, 1984), because it is the most reliable, but have modernized its seventeenth-century punctuation and orthography, except where they are the poet's own. All of the poems discussed, except one, are from the (relatively) undisputed Rochester canon, as established by Vieth in 1968. For all but one of Rochester's plays and his mountebank pamphlet, Frank H. Ellis's *John Wilmot, Earl of Rochester. The Complete Works* (London, 1994) is the chosen source. As Ellis does not include Rochester's obscene farce, *Sodom*, or even discuss his reasons for excluding it, Paddy Lyons's edition, *Rochester: Complete Poems and Plays* (London and Rutland, VT, 1993), is the only easily available source. In each case the quotation is identified by the editor's surname, page number and line number. I regret any inconvenience this procedure might occasion to readers searching for the same poems in their own editions, or even for the same lines, which may well have different numbers. When the new and genuinely complete edition by the great Rochester scholar Harold Love, of the University of Monash, Victoria, is finally in print, we may have something approaching a standard edition, but until then, and perhaps even then, Rochester's text will remain scattered and unstable.

Since completing this study *The Works of John Wilmot, Earl of Rochester* (Oxford, 1999) edited by the great Rochester scholar Harold Love has appeared. Impressive though its scholarship is its complexity and density, as well as its price, make it inaccessible to the majority of readers who will have to continue to use the library edition of Walker or the paperback editions of Ellis, Lyons or Vieth.

1

Introduction

In his famous study of the volume that appeared within weeks of the death of the poet John Wilmot, second Earl of Rochester, under the title *Poems on Several Occasions by the Right Honourable, the E. of R* ——— , David Vieth attributed fifteen of the poems in it to Rochester and eighteen poems to someone called 'Probably Rochester'.[1] Different editors have different ways of distinguishing between Rochester and 'Probably Rochester' or 'Possibly Rochester', none of them scientific or rigorous. Poems that are less than impressive are assumed to be unworthy of Rochester; Homer might nod, but not he, no matter how drunk or how ill he might have been. If Rochester could not have written all of a poem it is assumed that he must have written none of it.

Nowadays we assume that poems are written by individuals, usually lone individuals, and that if a poem is not by one single person it must be by another. Our scholarship and methods of discussion and recension cannot cope with the possibility that poems of merit could be by more than one person. We know from a contemporary satire that Rochester had disciples,[2] and it seems likely that Rochester had been a disciple in his turn; certainly he had imitators. To distinguish real Rochester from proto-Rochester or sub-Rochester is by now impossible, but all scholars, whether compiling concordances to Rochester or bibliographies of Rochester or discussing single poems, have no option but to assume a canon if they are to embark upon their self-imposed tasks at all. Twentieth-century literary study is more interested in poets than in poems and so, rather than seek Rochesterian poems, constructs a personage, Rochester.

In November 1679 Rochester is supposed to have written to Savile: 'I have sent you a libel in which my own share is not the least.'[3] The source for the letter is not unimpeachable, and the

1

dating is unlikely, but there is nothing unlikely in the idea of Rochester and the other court wits whiling away the long hours in the Whitehall withdrawing rooms by extemporizing – or pretending to extemporize – on themes or genres, or dittying together on familiar tunes. Understanding of Rochester's way of working is impossible without recognition of the readership that he sought among other noblemen and court wits, most of whom were involved from time to time in literary composition. Much of Rochester's versifying was done in company, with his companions' assistance or spurred on by competition with them. 'Possibly Rochester' might actually designate Rochester and John Grobham Howe, or Rochester and Buckhurst, and contrariwise 'Aphra Behn' could mean 'Aphra Behn and Rochester'. The best poets among Rochester's friends at court were Charles Sackville, Lord Buckhurst, better known nowadays by his later title as the sixth Earl of Dorset, George Villiers, second Duke of Buckingham, Sir George Etherege and Sir Charles Sedley. All four wrote poetry but very little can be securely attributed to any of them. Rochester is known to have collaborated too with very minor writers of the ilk of Robert Wolseley and Fleetwood Shepherd. A contemporary manuscript of Rochester's poem *Upon Nothing* divides the stanzas into three groups, the first six attributed to 'D: B:', the next nine to 'E: R:', and the last two to 'F: S:'.[4] This would mean little if the text were not carefully corrected in the hand of Rochester's mother.

The poet's personality is as difficult to establish as his text. His poetry adopts a vast range of personae of both sexes and of all ages. None of these voices should be assumed to be the voice of Rochester himself. When he died in 1680 at the age of 33, he was instantly mythologized by Gilbert Burnet in *Some Passages in the Life and Death of the Right Honourable John Earl of Rochester*. Burnet, chief apologist for the Whig cause, was pursuing his own politico-religious agenda, namely, 'the reforming a loose and lewd age' by the inculcation of whiggish morality. *Some Passages in the Life* is actually an interminable sermon addressed to a sick man, most of whose anguished questions his interlocutor did not quite understand. When Burnet met Rochester for the first time, in the autumn of 1679, the poet was already seriously ill; he did not see him again until he was dying.[5] Burnet's account exaggerates the disorderliness and irreligion of the poet's life in order to demonize a monarch who took money from the absolutist King of Catholic France so that he could rule without Parliament. Burnet's is a sober contribution to the vast and mostly uproarious propaganda campaign that created the impression of Charles's court as a supercharged bordello catering for all kinds of sexual preferences, including the criminal and bizarre, that endures to this day. Much of this anti-Stuart propaganda was bankrolled first by Buckingham, who was Marvell's patron, and subsequently by Buckhurst. In keeping with Burnet's sensationalist account of the poet's career was its companion volume, the compilation of poetry called *Poems on Several Occasions by the Right Honourable, the E. of R* ———. Rake Rochester was as effectively packaged and sold as any modern literary product. Both Burnet's memoir and the 1680 *Poems* were bestsellers, going through edition after edition over many years. In 1698 appeared a German translation of Burnet's memoir, in 1716 a French.

In 1682 Rochester's lifelong enemy, John Sheffield, Earl of Mulgrave, sought to topple him from his posthumous pre-eminence by vilifying him in *An Essay of Poetry*. To the end of his long life Mulgrave was obsessed by Rochester and determined to establish himself as Rochester's chief rival, inventing a symmetrical career for them both in defiance of the chronology that can be established from contemporary documentation. Mulgrave's attack in *An Essay of Poetry* inspired some of Rochester's friends, probably under the leadership and patronage of his half-niece, Anne Wharton, to join in vindicating his memory by bringing his *rifacimento* of Fletcher's *Valentinian* onto the stage and into print, with a long introduction by Robert Wolseley. Clearly Rochester's friends and family thought *Valentinian* significant; twentieth-century scholarship has tended to ignore this authenticated and extensive work while lavishing extraordinary and mostly pointless ingenuity on ephemeral squibs and versicles.

In 1691, irked by the continued success of as bad a piece of publishing as *Poems on Several Occasions by the Right Honourable, the E. of R* ———, Jacob Tonson put together a more respectable edition of Rochester's poetry, respectable unfortunately not only in the sense that the verse included had a better right to be considered as what Rochester actually wrote, but also in the sense that Tonson had suppressed what he considered

3

unsuitable for general readership. At the same time scabrous doggerel attributed to Rochester was being copied into hundreds of manuscript miscellanies. In 1695 letters purporting to have been written to Rochester by the deist Charles Blount were published in the posthumous edition of Blount's works prepared by his disciple Charles Gildon, a hack writer of the most desperate and the most ingenious, closely associated with John Toland whose forgeries of the documentation of the Old Cause remained unsuspected until our own time.[6] In 1697 nineteen personal letters from Rochester to Henry Savile were printed by Samuel Briscoe in the first volume of a collection of *Familiar Letters* edited by Tom Brown, quickly followed in the second volume edited by Charles Gildon by thirty-one letters from the poet to the actress Elizabeth Barry.[7] The bookseller, Samuel Briscoe, stated in a prefatory letter to the second volume that another collection of letters including 'fifty more of my Lord's and a considerable number of the Duke of Buckingham's and Sir George Etherege's' would be published in a third volume, which never appeared. If the letters had existed they would have been printed, if not by Briscoe then by the stationers who took over his properties after he was bankrupted in 1699. Jeremy Treglown, who edited Rochester's letters in 1980, accepted Briscoe's printings as genuine and struggled heroically to arrange them in a chronological order. He cannot be said to be entirely misguided, for it is as unlikely that all the letters printed by Briscoe are fake as that they are all genuine. Both Brown and Gildon could replicate any style or idiom; given three or four letters they would have had no difficulty whatsoever in producing a dozen or two that would seem to match. The syntax of the letters that survive in Rochester's holograph, almost all of them jotted on scraps of paper, is a coiled spring compared to the loose skeins of laddish chatter reproduced in *Familiar Letters*.

Briscoe printed both Rochester and spurious Rochester simply to make money. After the Bloodless Revolution the supporters of the King in exile used Rochester as propaganda, portraying him as the incarnation of all that was glamorous in the banished civilization of the Stuarts. Jacobite writers like Anne Finch, Countess of Winchilsea, harked back to the court of Charles II as the realm of true wit.

> You real wits who now contend
> With an ill-judging Age,
> Thus do you your Labours spend,
> Nor can Applause engage.
>
> In vain you wou'd sublimely write
> An Epigram, a Punn;
> A foul Burlesque gives more Delight,
> King Charles's days are done.[8]

Not content with recreating Rochester as the lord of wine and wit, the Jacobite propaganda machine endowed him with new fascination as the lord of love. In the thousands of scurrilous verses written in his lifetime to satirize his contemporaries at court in terms of their sexual proclivities Rochester was never mentioned as a performer, even in satires that accuse his known associates of orgiastic excesses of every hue. There was no evidence that he was any kind of sexual athlete until the Irish Jacobite Anthony Hamilton penned his fictionalized account of 'King Charles's days', published in 1713 as *Mémoires de la vie du Comte de Gramont*. Hamilton's version of Rochester as one whose all-conquering lust spared neither man, woman, nor child is still current. He had syphilis, we are told, though three of his four children lived healthily for as long as most people did in those days. Rochester's own testimony is that, 'of the three Buissnisses of this Age, Woemen, Polliticks & drinking', he and his friend Savile were 'Errant fumblers' in all but the third.[9] Eyewitnesses describe Rochester as tall and 'not a little too slender'; if he had been tubercular, the rigours of life in crowded, draughty, insanitary Whitehall would have been enough to kill him, without any superhuman feats of whoring and drinking. Failing hard facts drawn from documentary sources, scholars cannot resist treating selected poetry as autobiographical, though Rochester may no more be speaking *in propria persona* as 'The Maimed Debauchee' than he is as 'The Platonic Lady'. A man who writes about sex does not have to be a dedicated philanderer; the best war correspondents are seldom soldiers.

The next important contribution to the Rake Rochester myth is a letter St Evremond is supposed to have written to the Duchess of Mazarin, in which Rochester is credited with amours and masquerades that are lifted straight from the stock of the novella. Although St Evremond's editors have rejected the letter as spurious, Johannes Prinz and those who follow him persist in believing that, though not by St Evremond, the letter is by a contemporary who knew Rochester.[10] It is supposed to have been printed for the first time in 1702 in a publication listed by the nineteenth-century bibliographer, Lowndes, as *The Works of the Earl of Rochester and the Earl of Roscommon with their Lives prefixed, and the Delights of Venus now first published*, of which no exemplum is now known. Roscommon, who died in 1685, was a much more significant figure in Jacobite celebration of the court of Charles II than he ever was in life. The Rochester of the 'St Evremond' letter is invented by the same process. The synthetic Rochester proved an enduringly saleable product; editions of poems supposedly by Rochester that included the fake letter sold like hot cakes for seventy years.

By the time Johnson was writing his lives of the poets, in the 1770s, the Jacobite cause was totally discredited and with it, Rochester.

> Thus in a course of drunken gaiety, and gross sensuality, with intervals of study perhaps yet more criminal, with an avowed contempt of all decency and order, a total disregard of every moral, and a resolute denial of every religious obligation, he lived worthless and useless, and blazed out his youth and his health in lavish voluptuousness; till, at the age of one and thirty, he had exhausted the fund of life, and reduced himself to a state of weakness and decay.[11]

It is difficult to reconcile this useless and worthless individual with the man mourned by his step-niece, who grew up with him at Ditchley and Adderbury.

> Weep drops of blood my heart, thou'st lost thy pride,
> The cause of all thy hopes and fears, thy guide.
> He would have led thee right in wisdom's way
> .   .   .   .   .
> He civiliz'd the rude and taught the young,
> Made fools grow wise, such artful magic hung
> Upon his useful, kind, instructing tongue.[12]

Anne Wharton's elegy met an immediate response from Edmund Waller, Robert Wolseley and John Grobham Howe, all of whom had known Rochester. John Crowne's account of

6

Rochester as one who 'often supplies vulgar and necessitous wits wherewith to enrich themselves' is borne out by Nathaniel Lee and Sir Francis Fane.[13] Rochester did not often have spare cash to help poets, but he was prodigal with ideas and suggestions. He was also ready, as any gentleman was expected to be, to help uneducated women to express themselves in writing. One beneficiary was Aphra Behn, who described her reputation in 1680 as 'Fame himself first rais'd'.[14]

Writers attracted to Rochester's life have been unable or unwilling to brush away the accretion of speculation and opinion that has rendered their subject so glamorous in order to arrive at something truer to his life and circumstances. For *Lord Rochester's Monkey* Grahame Greene went so far as to acquire documents connected with Adderbury in the Restoration period and surely meant fully to research his subject, but what was published many years after his initial researches was an imaginative account of the life of a great sinner. The most recent biography, *So Idle a Rogue* by Jeremy Lamb, treats Rochester's life as a case history of chronic alcoholism, culminating in Wernicke's encephalopathy, dementia and death. Lamb seems unaware that to come drunk into the royal presence was a crime so heinous that in 1683 it resulted in the Duke of Albemarle's being sent to govern Jamaica. When the King drank everybody drank but no courtier could afford to get drunker than the King. As a Gentleman of the Bedchamber Rochester might well have had to supervise the carrying of the dead-drunk monarch to his bed; such scenes are described in *Valentinian* with great bitterness.

Though the facts of Rochester's life could be sorted out by the usual means adopted by serious historians, biographers of Rochester prefer their own insights to actual information, and often dispense with documentation altogether. Not only do they lack hard facts which could be found with more effort, they make assumptions that a better acquaintance with late-seventeenth-century mores and custom would reveal as improbable. Discussions of Rochester's marriage are invariably distorted by a thoroughly twentieth-century preoccupation with the question of whether or not he was 'in love with' his wife, while a crucial factor, namely the age of his wife, who was probably no more than 14 or 15 when he married her, is never investigated. The poet's liaison with Elizabeth Barry is described as a 'romance', his love for his friends is misunderstood and his relationship with his mother undervalued. His mother, under the name of his aunt, Lady St John, has even been charged by the mythologizers with burning Rochester's papers after his death. Rochester was closer than has often been realized to his uncle, Sir Walter St John, described by the court party as 'a rogue, anabaptist and a quaker'. Lady St John could have burnt any surviving correspondence between them because it was too dangerous to keep, especially after the accession of James II, whom both Rochester and his uncle had actively sought to exclude from the throne. Rochester's mother kept her own copies of her son's work; the only surviving manuscript of *Valentinian* contains a single correction of a copyist's mistake in her unmistakable hand, as well as swingeing elisions of all the lines relating to sodomy. She may well have been the source for many of Tonson's copies, for she did not die until 1696.

As short a discussion as this is cannot hope to outweigh the mass of inaccuracy, distortion and downright error that obscures the life and work of Rochester, but a concerted attempt will be made not to over-interpret sparse and contradictory evidence. All posthumous sources will be treated as unreliable unless contemporary documentation bears them out.

2

The Poet's Biography

Rochester is said to have been born on 1 April 1647. The only source for this date is John Gadbury's *Ephemeris, or a Diary* for 1695 that gives the poet's birth date as '1° April' and the place as Ditchley. As Gadbury had been publishing his *Ephemerides* every year since 1655 and did not include the poet's birth date before 1695, this source can have little authority. A child born at Ditchley should have been christened in the parish church at Spelsbury, but Rochester's christening does not appear in the parish record. For lack of better evidence Gadbury's date must stand. Certainly when Rochester first attended the House of Lords on 10 October 1667, having been summoned by a special writ on 29 July, he was understood to be 'in the twenty-first year of his age'.[1]

At the time of the poet's birth Ditchley Park was in the possession of the poet's mother, Anne, Baroness Wilmot, as the guardian of the infant proprietor, Sir Henry Lee, her first son by her first marriage. After the death of Sir Edward Henry Lee in 1639, several suitors had been proposed for the 25-year-old widow only to lose their lives in the fighting. In September 1643 it became known that she was to marry the royalist general, Henry Wilmot.[2] Wilmot, scion of an Oxfordshire family, had inherited the titles and the Irish estates of his father in May of that year, and was created Baron Wilmot of Adderbury in June 1643 for his services to the King at the battle of Roundway Down. He had been married for some months before, in mid-1644, he was found to be involved in a conspiracy to persuade Charles I to abdicate in favour of his son who, it was thought, would be more amenable than his father to the parliamentarians' demands.[3] Anne Wilmot was one of the St John family of Lydiard Tregoze, influential supporters of both the Crown and the rights of

Parliament, who would be deeply implicated in the coming struggle for a Protestant succession and limitation of the power of the monarch. It was the consolidation of the ranks of such presbyterian gentry during the ineffectual reign of 'Tumbledown Dick' Cromwell that made the Restoration possible.[4] For the St Johns and their ilk the Restoration was a time of optimism that gradually faded until they found themselves in the 1670s becoming once more opponents of the Crown.

During the Interregnum a good deal of influence remained in the hands of old country families whose agents and stewards often served as commissioners for compounding. In January 1645 the Committee of Sequestration reported that 'Anne Wilmot may enjoy her jointure to her own use only and not to the use of her husband'; by May of that year she had succeeded in bringing the Lee estates out of sequestration.[5] Somehow the spouses must have found time to be together in the summer of 1646 when their son John was conceived – unless the 'knowing men' who 'credibly informed' Anthony à Wood that the poet's father was not Henry Wilmot but his mother's cousin Sir Allen Apsley were telling the truth.[6] At the time of the poet's birth, Wilmot was in France.[7] In 1651 he was with the young King at the Battle of Worcester and was the only one of his officers allowed to accompany him on his tortuous escape from Boscobel. Safe in France in 1652, Wilmot was offered the title of Earl of Danby, which he refused, taking instead the title Earl of Rochester.[8]

In February 1654 Lady Rochester was granted a permit to travel 'beyond sea'. The immediate pretext was that she had to collect her two Lee sons from De Veau's academy in Paris, their governor having died of a virulent fever from which the boys were barely recovered, but she was also anxious to see her husband. When she arrived Rochester was in Germany raising money for the King[9] and, though she delayed her return until July and travelled back via Brussels in the hope of meeting him, there is no record that husband and wife actually met, let alone of the presence of their 7-year-old son at such a meeting.[10]

In 1658 Lord Rochester died. When John inherited the title he was a student at the grammar school in Burford, probably lodging in the town with one or other of his mother's attendant clergyman, perhaps Francis Giffard, as governor. On 24 February

1660, a few weeks before his thirteenth birthday, the young Earl left Ditchley for Wadham College.[11] Within four months his first effort at versifying was published in *Britannia rediviva*, a collection of Oxford verse celebrating the Restoration. Another Oxford publication of 1660, celebrating Henrietta Maria's recovery from illness, carried two more loyalist poems signed by Rochester, a tribute 'To her sacred Majesty the Queen Mother' and a Latin poem 'Impia Blasphemi'. Anthony à Wood noted that 'these three copies were made, as 'twas then well known, by Robert Whitehall a physician of Merton college, who pretended to instruct the count (then twelve years of age) in the art of poetry'.[12] The poems produced the intended result: the King granted Rochester a pension of £500 a year.[13]

In September 1661 Rochester donned scarlet robes to receive a kiss on the cheek and the degree of Master of Arts from the hands of Edward Hyde, now Chancellor of the University and Earl of Clarendon. Within two months, the Countess had packed her boy off on a tour of the continent in the company of another doctor, Alexander Balfour.[14] The grand tour seldom took more than a year or so; Rochester's travels in southern Europe went on for more than three years. The combination of the length of his sojourn and the choice of a physician for his governor suggests that he was travelling for health. By the time he saw England again, at the end of 1664, his mother had had Adderbury fully restored and furnished to a pitch of magnificence that drove her financial advisers to despair. What was more she had been appointed Groom of the Stole to Clarendon's daughter Anne Hyde, now Duchess of York. At court or in the country Anne Rochester lived, in her steward's phrase, 'as the top of all', sublimely unmindful of any shortfall between income and expenditure.[15] She taught the same cavalier attitude towards money to her son. What both had they spent, whether it was theirs to spend or not. Neither considered that debts were for paying. The people who acted for them were often constrained to use their own securities in servicing their employers' debts; ten years after Rochester's death his steward John Cary was still being besieged by the poet's creditors whenever he dared to show his face in London.[16]

On his return from his European tour Rochester presented himself at Whitehall with a letter for the King from his beloved sister Henriette, and so began his career as a courtier.[17] As a successful career at court would require funds which the Wilmot estates could not furnish, an advantageous match had to be made and that without delay. While her son was still abroad Anne Rochester's choice had lighted on Elizabeth Malet, sole heiress to the vast wealth of John Malet of Enmore; by the time Rochester returned to England his mother had secured the assistance of the King, the Chancellor and Lady Castlemaine in promoting the match. Unmoved, the lady's trustees persisted in rather slow-moving negotiations for a match with the heir of the Earl of Sandwich.[18] The Countess decided upon a pre-emptive strike.[19] On the evening of 26 May 1665, as Miss Malet travelled with her grandfather in his coach through Charing Cross, a group of 'both horse and foot-men' stopped the coach, snatched the girl and bundled her into another vehicle, which set off at high speed. She was successfully conveyed to a secret rendez-vous, but the intended bridegroom was arrested before he could reach her, an outcome that must have been brought about by Rochester's own indiscretion compounded by failure to act with sufficient decisiveness to drive off the plebeians sent to intercept him. His petition to the King, pleading 'Inadvertency' as well as the conventional 'Ignorance in ye Law and Passion' as the occasion of the offence, is less an apology for having attempted the marriage by capture than for having failed to pull it off.[20]

For three weeks, as plague raged in London, the poet languished in the Tower.[21] He was released only to be sent on another venture designed to finance his court career, this time as a member of Sandwich's expedition to plunder the Dutch fleet then anchored off the Norwegian coast. Sandwich put the young Earl, who had been provided by his mother with too little money to pay for his keep and other necessaries, in a cabin aboard his flagship, *Revenge*. The engagement was a disaster; 118 of the British force were killed and 239 wounded. Rochester wrote dutifully to his mother, signing himself her 'most obedient son', delineating the danger in no more words than it took him to say that, although he had been very careful with his money, he had been obliged to borrow.[22] He remained with the fleet for a few weeks more, then returned to Whitehall.

On 31 October 1665 the King came to Rochester's aid with a gift of £750.[23] On 21 March 1666, after the court had returned to

London from Oxford where it had removed to escape the Great Plague, Rochester was made a Gentleman of the Bedchamber with a salary of £1,000 a year which, supposing the merry monarch troubled to pay it, was nowhere near enough to finance the dress and equipage for one in a position of such glamour and eminence.[24] A Gentleman of the Bedchamber, who was provided with accommodation in one set or other of Whitehall's 2,000 rooms, was obliged to sleep in the King's bedroom one week of every quarter, and to wait upon him at table when he dined in his chamber. If the Groom of the Stole was unavailable to supervise the King's dressing in the morning, a Gentleman of the Bedchamber would be called upon to stand in for him. The rest of the time Rochester made up one of the company standing, waiting about and dancing attendance in the Whitehall drawing rooms, ready to provide entertaining company should the King desire it. In April and October the court removed to Newmarket for the races, which were accompanied by all kinds of field sports. At first Rochester went too, but later he took the twice-yearly trips to Newmarket as opportunities to escape from the duties of attendance.

In June 1666, when the court went on its summer perambulation, Rochester went to sea again under Sir Edward Spragge against De Ruyter. This time he covered himself with glory by volunteering to carry a message and bring back an answer in a small boat, in the thick of heavy fire that had already inflicted appalling damage on the English fleet. Not long after he returned to court he learned that after many vicissitudes Miss Malet's match with Viscount Hinchinbrooke was finally off, the young man having discovered when he attended her at Tunbridge that summer that he misliked 'the vanity and liberty' of her carriage.[25] Miss Malet contrived to shock even Samuel Pepys, who wrote in his diary for 25 November 1666:

> I will remember that Mr Ashburnham today at dinner told how the rich fortune Mrs Mallett reports of her servants: that my lord Herbert would have had her – my Lord Hinchinbrooke was indifferent to have her – my Lord Jo. Butler might not have her – my Lord of Rochester would have forced her and Sir Francis Popham (who nevertheless is likely to have her) would kiss her breech to have her.[26]

Sir Francis Popham did not have her. On the morning of 29 January 1667, in the royal chapel at Whitehall, without the knowledge or consent of her guardians, Elizabeth Malet was married to Rochester and bedded immediately afterwards 'to make sure work of it'. That evening Anne Rochester gave 'a great supper' for the King and the Duke of York and 'much company'.[27]

Though the lady was secured, her fortune was not, no settlement having been agreed.[28] The Malet trustees, led by the bride's grandfather, Lord Hawley, had no intention of giving the disposal of the estate into the hands of the Rochesters.[29] After the wedding Elizabeth stayed with Rochester in London until April, when Anne Rochester accompanied the couple, first to visit their Lee in-laws at Ditchley, and then to Adderbury, where Elizabeth was to make her home under the tutelage of her mother-in-law, whose duties as Groom of the Stole would keep her in attendance on the Duchess of York for most of the year.[30] In the summers, when Anne Rochester was likely to be in the country, Rochester and Elizabeth would travel to Somerset for the yearly review of the management of the Malet estates. At first, while he still had hopes of getting the Malet estate for his own use, Rochester wooed his bride with all his considerable charm, but it was not long before his letters from London grew shorter and more rallying in tone as sweet talk was replaced by the politeness that was all a well-bred husband owed his wife.

Young as Elizabeth Rochester almost certainly was, she realized that the way to her husband's heart was through poetry. Bound with Rochester's holograph texts in Portland MS PwV 31 are drafts of poems in Elizabeth's hand. In eight manuscripts we may find attributed to Rochester a 'Song' beginning:

> Give me leave to rail at you.
> I ask nothing but my due,
> To call you false, and then to say,
> You shall not keep my heart a day,
> But (alas!) against my will,
> I must be your captive still.
> Ah! be kinder then, for I
> Cannot change, and would not die.

(Walker, 20)

These eight lines were printed as a song in *Songs for i 2 & 3 Voyces Composed by Henry Bowman* in 1677; in three of the eight manuscripts this and a following stanza are conflated with two more stanzas of a song in the same metre, beginning 'Nothing adds to your fond fire'. These plus a third stanza are to be found in one of the Portland MSS in the hand of Elizabeth Rochester and are usually taken to be of her composition. Perhaps Rochester and his wife sat down to ditty together; each may have had a hand in the other's verse.

After his marriage Rochester's court career gathered momentum, despite his growing intimacy with the Duke of Buckingham. When Buckingham fled the court under suspicion of treason, and succeeded in evading capture for the ensuing four months, Rochester took his turn as Gentleman of the Bedchamber.[31] In June he was commissioned as a captain in Prince Rupert's regiment and in July he was one of several under-age peers summoned by a special writ to take his seat in the depopulated House of Lords.[32] The Lords protested. Rochester delayed his appearance until Parliament met on 10 October 1667 and went on to attend twenty-three days of the session. When Clarendon's impeachment was debated, Rochester took Buckingham's side against his old friend so far as to sign the declaration of dissent, which was to be presented in the event that the Lords failed to comply with the vote of the Commons for Clarendon's imprisonment.[33] Meanwhile he was collecting court appointments: on 28 February 1668 he received the warrant of gamekeeper for the County of Oxford; in April he petitioned for the grant of the offices in the four bailiwicks of Wychwood Forest, in his mother's interest as the widow of Sir Edward Henry Lee.

In the late summer of 1668 Elizabeth Rochester conceived; as her pregnancy progressed Rochester involved himself in a series of scrapes. On 2 December Pepys was scandalized to hear the King regale the distinguished company with a story of Rochester's 'having of his clothes stole while he was with a wench, and his gold all gone but his clothes found afterward stuffed into a feather-bed by the wench that stole them'.[34] At a dinner for the Dutch Ambassador on 16 February Rochester was so annoyed by Thomas Killigrew's taunting him for keeping his wife in the country that he fetched him a blow on the ear in the presence of the King.[35] The King caused scandal not only by failing to chastise Rochester but by allowing himself to be seen the next day walking familiarly with him.[36] In less than a month Rochester was in trouble again; he was heard to say such 'ugly slighting thinges' of the King while visiting his friend Savile, who was then a prisoner in the Tower, that he was challenged to a duel.[37] The matter was hushed up mainly by sending Rochester off to Paris on 12 March with a letter to the King's sister Henriette, who was helping in the secret negotiations that would culminate in the Treaty of Dover. Rochester left so precipitately he did not visit his wife, who was expected soon to lie in, though his mother begged him to.[38] On 28 April, after a difficult labour, Elizabeth bore a lusty daughter who was christened Anne after her grandmother.[39] Elizabeth was so ill after the birth that her attendants feared she might die, but by 6 May she was fully recovered and Rochester apparently with her, for his steward reports in a letter of that date that, being 'not yet willing to part with her Head', Elizabeth persuaded him to defer indefinitely a business trip to London.[40] It seems that Rochester was subsequently sent back to Paris, where he got into a fight at the Opera in August.[41]

When Parliament reconvened on 19 October Rochester was back in England and attended half a dozen times before the Lords received notice from the King that a duel was to be fought between Rochester and John Sheffield, the young Earl of Mulgrave. Rochester being his servant, the King said, he knew 'what course to take with him' but, as both miscreants were members of the House, he suggested that the matter would be best handled there. The next day the Usher of the Black Rod brought in Mulgrave, sat him in his place for the first time and told him to proceed no further in the matter of the duel. On 26 November, Rochester being in his place, he was asked to give his undertaking that he would not fight, to which he replied sweetly that he had never been angry with the Earl of Mulgrave.[42] The account of this affair that Mulgrave went on publishing to the end of his long life in order to discredit Rochester is not borne out in any particular by the documentary record.

At the end of March 1670 Rochester borrowed £400, half of it from rents due to his half-nieces, the Lee heiresses, who were wards of his mother.[43] At the beginning of May, when he and his lady set out on their yearly visit to Somersetshire, Elizabeth was once more pregnant.[44] In July Rochester wrote to her at Adderbury from lodgings in Lincoln Inn Fields, in 'the house next to the Dukes playhouse in Portugall Row', apologizing for writing so seldom.

I thanke you for my cheeses, my sugar of roses, & all my good things, pray lett it not be necessary for mee to put you too often in mind of what you ought not to bee less forward in doing than I in advising, I hope you will give me noe occasion to explain my selfe, for if I am putt upon that you will find mee very troublesome, I receiv'd no letter from you wth an inclos'd to y^r mother nor doe I beleive you writt any...[45]

On 22 July John Cary wrote to Sir Ralph Verney from his house at Woodstock:

I understand by Mr Hill that my Lord Rochester hath had a little misfortune at play & lost his money so as he borrowed 200^l of Mr Hill which his Lo^{pp} acknowledgeth being now at my house with his Lady, who hath lately had the measles heare but is now very well againe. His Lo^{pps} further desire is that you would give consent that Mr Hill doe lend him 300^l more to make up his sume 500^l which he sayes Mr Hill will doe if we consent.[46]

Gambling was another of the courtier's inescapable duties that Rochester could ill afford. He attended Parliament but rarely, aware perhaps that the exhaustive discussions of raising revenue to equip a fleet against France were entirely pointless, as the King had signed the secret treaty of Dover months before. At the end of November, under pressure to pay off some of his debts, he fee-farmed a rent of £100 per annum for the rather high price of £2,000, of which he had already had – and almost certainly spent – £1,500.[47] He was at Adderbury for the birth of his son in December 1670, where he had leisure to write, among other things, witty letters to his friends. Sedley and Buckhurst agreed to stand as godfathers.

In the ensuing months life at Adderbury became much more difficult for Elizabeth. On 26 March 1671, Anne Hyde died. Once Anne Rochester had supervised her mistress's laying-out and accompanied her to her last resting place, she and her Lee granddaughters withdrew into Oxfordshire. As she was providing most of the finance for Adderbury out of her own considerable income and the rents of her Lee granddaughters' estates, Anne Rochester felt no qualms in taking over the reins as *châtelaine* and throwing Adderbury open for the balls and parties that would lead up to the marriage of Eleanor Lee with their neighbour Lord Norreys.[48] Elizabeth wrote to Rochester in London telling him of her intention to move to her own house at Enmore, in which she was apparently supported by her mother-in-law. He replied with chilling sarcasm.

> You have order'd the matter soe well that you must of necessity bee attt the place you intend before I can give you an answer to y^r letter, methinks you ought rather to have resolv'd in the negative since it was wh^t I desir'd of you before, but the happy conjunction of my mother and you can produce nothing but extreme good carriage to mee as it has formerly done; you shew y^r selfe very discreet and kind in this as in other matters, I wish you very well, & my mother, but assure you, I will bee very backward in giving you the trouble of
>
> Your humble servant
Rochester[49]

He was to be as good as his word.

Anne Rochester and her Lee granddaughters had been looking for a house of their own but matters were complicated by negotiations for the wedding of Eleanor Lee, which necessitated the drawing of accounts for the management of the Lee girls' estate, to which both Anne Rochester and her son owed considerable sums of money. Rochester's poverty was the more acute because he could not encash the payment orders for his salary as a Gentleman of the Bedchamber. By March 1672 he was owed £3,375.[50] Elizabeth's attempt to transfer her household to Somerset failed; within weeks she requested her husband's permission to return to Adderbury, which she found as uncongenial as ever. Rochester's response to her complaints was withering:

> Madam,
> It was the height of Complyance forc't mee to agree y^r La^{SP} shoult come into Oxfordshire if it does not please you 'tis not my fault, though much my expectation; I receive the Compliment you make in desiring my company as I ought to doe; But I have a poore living to gett that I may bee less Burdesome to y^r La^{SP}; if y^r La^{SP} had return'd moneys out of Somerts for the Buying those things you sent for they myght have been had by this time ... [51]

In June 1671 Rochester was in Bath; in July he and his wife and daughter travelled into Somerset. He was at Adderbury again in September.

By mid-December he was 'forbid the court againe about publishing (or rather not concealing) a Libell, wherin the Duchesse of Cleveland and Mr Churchill & others were concerned'.[52] The libel in question was probably 'Mistress Knight's Advice to the Duchess of Cleveland in Distress for a Prick'.

> Quoth the Duchess of Cleveland to Councillor Knight,
> 'I'd fain have a prick knew I how to come by't,
> But you must be secret and give your advice –
> Though cunt be not coy, reputation is nice.'

> 'To some cellar in Sodom, your Grace must retire,
> Where porters with black-pots sit round the coal fire.
> There open your case and your Grace cannot fail
> Of a dozen of pricks for a dozen of ale.'

> 'Say you so!' quoth the Duchess. 'Ay, by God!' quoth the whore.
> 'Then give me the key that unlocks the back door.
> I'd rather be fucked by porters and carmen,
> Than thus be abused by Churchill and Jermyn.'

(Walker, 61)

This lampoon survives in four contemporary manuscripts and was printed by the unknown collector of *Poems on Several Occasions by the Right Honourable, the E of R——*. The King took an extremely dim view of lampoons on his mistresses; Rochester had not been readmitted to the royal presence before he was involved in 'a foolish quarrel in a playhouse' with the son of Lord Newport.[53] He was to be involved in dozens of similar skirmishes over the following years. In contrast to his other reputed vices, Rochester's belligerence is amply supported by contemporary documentation.

Rochester may not even have noticed the publishing of two poems of his in a volume called *A Collection of Poems, Written upon Several Occasions, by Several Persons* early in 1672, for in February he was once more in disgrace. In the first week of July, accompanied by his wife and 3-year-old daughter, he travelled into the west.[54] In September he was ill and obliged to pawn his plate to pay his doctors' fees. He wrote an amusing description of his treatment to his wife, but even this fact has not been sufficient to warn his biographers that his disease was probably not venereal.[55] Sick people could not remain in proximity to the King at Whitehall; it was probably during his convalescence and the welcome suspension of his court duties that Rochester began to interest himself in theatre. On 21 March 1673 he was summoned to the House of Lords upon suspicion of his involvement in an intended duel with Viscount Dunbar; he was in his place the next day to be bound over, and attended every day until the adjournment on 29 March. Dryden chose this moment to write to Rochester, thinking to gain his favour by not only flattering him outrageously but also deriding Buckingham. If Rochester deigned to send an answer, Dryden had the good sense to destroy it. In his letter Dryden noted that Rochester had withdrawn himself from attendance, 'the curse of Courts'; indeed, it is difficult to find evidence of his being in regular attendance at court after this date. In one of his letters to his wife he quoted Cowley from memory (hence inaccurately):

> Is there a man yee Gods, whome I doe hate
> Dependence & Attendance bee his fate
> Lett him bee busy still & in a crowde
> And very much a slave & very proud[56]

In the summer of 1673 the perpetual Restoration crisis took a new and ominous turn. An army was mustered on Blackheath, under the command of the Duke of York, ostensibly to invade Holland but more obviously to cow opposition to pro-Catholic royal policy by making a display of military might. Rochester's friend Henry Savile became known at court as the author of 'Advice to a Painter to Draw the Duke by', a satire in the anti-Yorkist genre invented by Andrew Marvell. Buckingham, Marvell's patron, was recruiting in Yorkshire, where, despite his popularity, the people would not come to his standard until he had taken the sacrament publicly with his officers from the hands of the Archbishop of York, as an assurance of his adherence to the Protestant cause.

In the autumn of 1673 the gossips said that Rochester, fearing that the King would 'slacken his kindness to him', was cursing his mother for ignoring the King's express wish and arranging a marriage of her granddaughter Anne Lee with the son of one of the King's most outspoken adversaries. His anxiety was groundless, for in February the King granted him the Rangership of Woodstock, in the interest of his mother, who had a claim on the Rangership as the widow of Sir Edward Henry Lee and guardian of his heirs. The grant, the reversion of which was to go to Anne's grandson, Sir Edward Henry Lee, was part of the negotiations for a match between him and the King's favourite daughter, Charlotte Fitzroy, who were to be Stewards and

Farmers of Woodstock.[57] Anne Rochester may have entered into these negotiations primarily in the hope of doing something for Rochester, because the match was well understood to be a disaster for the Lees, the Lee estates being desperately in need of an injection of capital, which nobody expected from the King. The situation regarding the offices at Woodstock was confused; months of acrimonious legal quibbling followed the transfer of the Rangership to Rochester. The Rangership brought with it a stipend (though there was no guarantee that the King would pay it), numerous opportunities for lucrative patronage, and the right to stay at High Lodge. High Lodge being a hunting lodge, consisting of a banqueting hall, with the usual offices, stabling, kennels, guard-rooms and gun-rooms, and a minimum of sleeping accommodation, there was never any question that Elizabeth Rochester, her children and their entourage would make their home there.

In the summer of this year or the next the poet is thought to have departed from his custom of staying with his wife's grandfather in Bath on his way to Somerset and gone with other fashionable folk to Tunbridge Wells, where he wrote the verse satire of which a version was published in 1675 in Richard Head's *Proteus Redivivus*. As 'Tunbridge Wells' is one of the most confused texts associated with Rochester and exhibits all the signs of gradual accretion by several hands, it cannot be said to provide incontrovertible evidence that the poet was writing from his own observation. In December Rochester was called upon to act as second for Savile, who had been challenged by Mulgrave after reviling him in the presence of the King.[58] As the Duke of York had by this time prevailed with the King to forbid Savile's presence at court, Rochester found himself once more identified as an opponent of the succession.

The order of events in the ensuing months is not easy to establish. Rochester's liaison with Elizabeth Barry may have begun as early as 1675, but it seems unlikely. In the spring he must have been with Elizabeth because their fourth and last child, Malet, was baptized on 6 January the next year. In June 1675, after 'deboshing all night with the King', Rochester, Buckhurst, Lord Sussex and Henry Savile were passing through the Privy Garden when they happened upon the elaborate set of sundials and chronometers that the Jesuit Franciscus Linus had constructed for the King. Someone shouted, 'Kings and kingdoms tumble down and so shalt thou', and within seconds the structure was in smithereens.[59] In August and September Rochester was ill once more and withdrew to the country.

It was at this time that Rochester began writing for the stage; his first effort was a scene for a play by Sir Robert Howard. This was followed by new scenes for Fletcher's tragedy *Valentinian* and the accompanying farce *Sodom*. From February to April 1676 he was once more in disgrace and once more in the country. Meanwhile three of his songs, one exalting the pleasures of the bottle over sex, another 'Against Constancy' and the last beginning 'While on those lovely looks I gaze' appeared, unattributed, in *A New Collection of the Choicest Songs*, licensed in April 1676. In the summer he is supposed to have led a riotous gang of revellers at Woodstock, where his new accomplice in crime was the oppositionist tearaway Lord Lovelace, whose escapades were, if anything, wilder than Rochester's. The Stuart administration was now facing a serious threat as leaders of the Lords increased the pressure for the exclusion of a Catholic from the succession. The frolicking at Woodstock may have disguised graver matters. On 17 June Rochester, together with William Jephson, Sir George Etherege, Captain Bridges and a Mr Downs, were involved in a fracas at Epsom, which ended in the death of Downs 'by his hurts recd from ye Rusticks'.[60] In late August and early September, while he was staying with his wife and mother at Adderbury, Rochester paid visits to the Earl of Anglesey and the Earl of Clarendon.[61] These meetings may have been purely social, but both men were important if discreet supporters of a Protestant succession.

On 15 February 1677, when Parliament reassembled after a fifteen-month prorogation, in the hope of forcing a new election, Buckingham argued in the House of Lords with great wit and passion that the prorogation had been unlawful and that Parliament was effectively dissolved. The motion failed. Buckingham, Shaftesbury, Wharton and Salisbury were committed to the Tower. Shaftesbury whiled away his time by listing the supporters of the various factions; against John Wilmot, Earl of Rochester, he entered 'w' for 'worthy', signifying a supporter of the Old Cause. Now for the first time Rochester began to take his duties as a member of the House of Lords seriously. He sat on the committee set up to deal with the publisher and printer of *The Growth of Popery and Arbitrary Government in England*, a pamphlet by Marvell that argued as Buckingham had done that the fifteen-month prorogation was unlawful. He went on to attend the house for twenty-three of its fifty-five sittings. In April, at the same time that he was petitioning for a share in the huge tracts of land at the King's disposal in Ireland for himself, he acted as a trustee for Nell Gwyn, to whom the King had granted some disputed Irish lands.[62] He joined Nell Gwyn, Buckhurst and the rest of 'the merry gang' to petition for Buckingham's release.[63] When in July Buckingham was at last allowed to leave the Tower 'for a month's air', he stayed in Rochester's lodgings at Whitehall, preparing his submissions to the King, until he was obliged to seek more suitable accommodation.[64] When in August the King pardoned him, Buckingham wrote several times to Rochester at Woodstock; in October he offered to bring his famous pack of hounds.[65] At some point it was suggested that Monmouth visit Woodstock. None of these visits seems to have eventuated, for Rochester had fallen 'exseeding ill'.[66] In December, when the actress Elizabeth Barry bore his child and called her Hester, Rochester was still at Woodstock.[67] Meanwhile more samples of Rochester's writing were appearing in print. The wonderful song beginning 'All my past life is mine no more' was printed in *Songs for i 2 & 3 Voyces* of 1677. A mildly pornographic song appeared in two printed anthologies of 1677, *The Wits Academy: or, The Muses Delight* and *The Last and Best Edition of New Songs*, and was reprinted in another collection the next year and the year after.

If Rochester recovered from the October spell of illness, it was not for long. A new bout laid him low at Adderbury from April to June of the following year. In September 1678 there was a falling-out between Rochester, his neighbour Lord Lovelace and his brother-in-law Lord Norreys, 'even to Blowes and drawing of swords'.[68] His interest in politics continued to grow.

> A considerable time before his last Sickness, his Wit began to take a more serious Bent; and to frame and fashion it selfe to publick Business; he began to informe himself of the Wisdom of our Laws and the excellent Constitution of the *English* Government and to speak in the house of Peers with general approbation...[69]

In mid-November 1678 Rochester reappeared in the House of Lords and attended almost every remaining day of the sitting, but he was not there to take the oath of supremacy on 30 November, and was obliged to take it on 4 December instead. He attended on only three of the twenty days of the sitting thereafter. When Parliament reconvened on 6 March 1679 Rochester was present and attended on all but sixteen of the sixty-seven days that the House sat before the dissolution in May.

Meanwhile the slow trickle of Rochester's works appearing in print had become a stream of broadsides hawked about the streets. Two versions of *Upon Nothing* appeared, two versions of *Artemisa to Cloe*, a shortened version of *A Satire against Mankind* and *A Very Heroical Epistle from my Lord All-Pride to Dol-Common*. In December, when Dryden was set upon and severely beaten in Rose Alley, suspicion lighted on Rochester, who seems for once to have had no hand in the business. By the end of the year Rochester's health was failing so fast he probably should have placed himself under his mother's care at Adderbury. He was at Westminster for the opening of Parliament on 27 January but returned immediately to Woodstock. On 3 February John Cary reported to Sir Ralph Verney that a huge fire Rochester had made to air the house had almost burnt High Lodge down; 'it was saved by much help yet not without much damage'.[70] Even so Rochester did not remove to Adderbury. In the early spring he was in London, where Burnet met him on several occasions, but he soon returned to High Lodge where, in an excess of febrile high spirits, he suddenly felt fit enough to set out on the gruelling ride to Enmore, only to collapse and be brought back by coach.

On 1 June Rochester's steward wrote to Sir Ralph Verney:

> I much feare my Lord Rochester hath not long to live, he is heare at his lodg & his mother my lady dowager & his lady are with him. And doctor skirt of london & doctor radcliffe of oxon Himselfe is now very weake, God Allmighty restore him if it be his will for he is growne to be the most altered Pson, the most devout & pious pson as I generally ever knew

Unable to rebel in any other way, Elizabeth Rochester had become a Catholic, to the great dismay of her family and of the Rochesters.

> And further what is much comfort to my Lady dowager & us all in this sorrow is. His lady is returnd to her first love the protestant religion and on sunday last received the sacrament with her lord, & hath bin at prayer with us[71]

By 15 June the word went out for a milch ass for Rochester and within a day or two he had 'milch asses sufficient'.[72] He seemed 'on the mending hand' though his condition was still very unstable:

> pretty good dayes succeed ill nights, which help to keep upp his spirits, but he is very weake, and expresses himselfe very goode

On 19 June he signed a remonstrance, witnessed by his mother and Robert Parsons, in which he abjured people 'no more to deny' the existence of God, 'or his Providence or despise his goodness; no more to make a mock of Sin, or contemn the pure and excellent Religion'. To a modern mind Rochester had simply questioned the grounds of religious belief, but his contemporaries did not allow themselves to do even that. Wavering and backsliding were considered as appalling as downright denial, and far graver than disorderly sexuality or habitual intemperance. The poet's decline from then on was gradual and fairly uneventful. He developed ugly sores on his back, almost certainly pressure sores rather than the syphilitic buboes of legend. On 26 June Anne Rochester wrote a letter, supposedly at the poet's dictation, begging Burnet to visit his deathbed. Burnet did not arrive at Woodstock until 20 July. By then the poet was reported 'very weak and ill, drawing near his last'. On 22 July he was 'pretty well' but 'grew ill towards night'. On 24 July Burnet left him; on 26 July at 2 in the morning he died. The next day, in the presence of his mother, his wife and the faithful John Cary, his will was read. Elizabeth Rochester must have listened with a sinking heart as she heard:

> for the better assurance of a happie correspondencie between my deare mother and my deare wife, I doe appoint to my mother and wife the gardianshipp of my sonn till he attaine the age of one and twentie, soe long as my wife shall remaine unmarried and friendlily live with my mother...[73]

At the poet's funeral on 9 August the sermon was preached by Robert Parsons. It went instantly into print, bound up with Burnet's account of the poet's life, to be sold up and down the country as an object lesson in the corrupting influence of an ungoverned monarch.

3

The Poet at Court

The court of Charles II was modelled in part on that of Louis XIV at the Louvre where Henrietta Maria had lived in exile. Like his uncle, Charles kept an ensemble of twenty-four violinists to accompany French dances and a company of French players to perform French plays. The court ladies wore French fashions. Charles, less concerned with pomp and ceremony than Louis and far less tolerant of boredom, required from the inner circle of his courtiers not French formality and adulation but entertainment, grace and a well-bred easiness of carriage. Rochester responded as any clever teenager would, by showing off the readiness and extravagance of his wit, which at first the King appreciated even when the joke went against him.

Most important among Rochester's rivals for the King's attention was the King's childhood playfellow, George Villiers, second Duke of Buckingham. As a new Gentleman of the Bedchamber 19-year-old Rochester must have been impressed by the elegance and panache of 38-year-old Buckingham, who had been a legend ever since he danced the Element of Fire in Benserade's *Masque Royale de la Nuit* at the court of Louis XIV in 1658.[1] Years after Buckingham's death Burnet, no admirer of courtiers, remembered that he had 'a flame in his wit' that was inimitable. Amid his multifarious involvements as politician, military commander, courtier, privy councillor and minister of state, Buckingham cared passionately about literature and spent what leisure he had discussing problems of literary taste and working on literary projects. Rochester can have seen little of him in his early months at Whitehall, but they were soon friends, as may be seen by Buckingham's letter asking Rochester to wait on the King and lie in the royal bedchamber in his place:

I am very perticular in ths matter that your Lordship may see I am a man of businesse, and take the liberty of troubling you upon this occasion becawse I had rather bee oblidged to you then any body else.[2]

Though Buckingham was the best-known wit of the generation before Rochester's, very few works can be ascribed to him with any confidence. His role seems to have been that of instigator, suggesting topics that his fellow wits might extemporize upon, judging, classifying and improving their efforts. In 1667 he completed his adaptation of *The Chances*, which was played in a double bill with Dryden's *Secret Love*. Dryden replied to Buckingham's epilogue apologizing for his 'fag-end of a play' by using the prologue to his next play, *Albumazor*, to vilify him. The skirmish became a war when Buckingham recast *The Rehearsal*, originally intended as an attack on Davenant and Howard, as an attack on Dryden, whom he called 'Old Bayes' in reference to his appointment as laureate in 1668. Though Rochester was slow to join the anti-Dryden faction, he was to become the principal chastiser of Dryden's time-serving careerism.

It was possibly through Buckingham that Rochester made the acquaintance of Charles Sackville, Lord Buckhurst, whom he would have known and perhaps envied as the author of the enormously popular lyric 'To all you ladies now on land', which Buckhurst is supposed to have dashed off the night before the great naval battle of 3 June 1664, in which he fought with distinction. Rochester would have witnessed too Buckhurst's facility in penning love-songs which combined the purest diction with a complex ironic tone. As he wrote in 'An Allusion to Horace':

> For pointed satires I would Buckhurst choose,
> The best good man, with the worst natured muse,
> For songs and verses mannerly obscene,
> That can stir nature up by springs unseen,
> And, without forcing blushes, warm the queen...
>
> (Walker, 101, ll. 59–63)

By the time he wrote these lines Rochester had been imitating Buckhurst's 'mannerly obscene' with such success that he had eclipsed his master. Though Buckhurst was often at Whitehall, he held no court appointment and was not obliged, as Rochester was, to dance attendance on the King at all hours of the day and night. His friend Sir Charles Sedley came and went as freely and Rochester admired and perhaps envied him almost as much.

> Sedley has that prevailing gentle art,
> That can with a resistless charm impart
> The loosest wishes to the chastest heart,
> Raise such a conflict, kindle such a fire,
> Betwixt declining virtue and desire,
> Till the poor vanquished maid dissolves away,
> In dreams all night, in sighs and tears all day.
>
> (Walker, 101, ll. 64–70)

During the Interregnum elegant and disabused amorous lyrics had been deployed as touchstones by which to measure the dreariness of republican sexual culture, which was no less lecherous than anything before or since, but vastly more hypocritical and oppressive. The Cavaliers considered that Puritan mores exalted workaday reproductive sex at the expense of intelligent management of polymorphous pleasure. Carew had predicted in his 'Elegy upon the Death of the Dean of St Pauls' (first published in 1633) that Donne's 'strict laws' would be 'Too hard for libertines in poetry'. The Restoration poets followed the Cavaliers in devoutly striving to disprove Carew's prediction.

The most important clue to Rochester's way of working is Portland MS PwV 31, which contains the only versions of Rochester poems in his own hand. This is a slim volume, in which half sheets and scraps of paper have been carefully mounted. Some of these bear unmistakable signs of having been folded several times until they were not much bigger than modern postage stamps, quite small enough to be slipped easily into the fob of the stiffest, tightest court waistcoat. One poem has been written across a fold, as if held in the palm of a hand. Another has been folded before the ink was dry. A courtier in attendance might not sit without the King's permission, but in all the withdrawing rooms at Whitehall there would have been a standish with pen and ink where the poet, seeing an opportunity, could take out his paper and quickly jot down the lines that had been forming in his mind. Only two of the nine poems or fragments of poems in Rochester's holograph are known to us from other sources. If seven of these scraps of paper had not survived we would have no inkling that Rochester had ever written anything like them. The two stanzas of hyperbolic panegyric beginning ''Twas a dispute 'twixt heav'n and Earth', that celebrate a beauty so dazzling that had the poet seen her eyes he 'must have perished in that first surprize', are unlike anything otherwise attributed to Rochester. Another, beginning 'Leave this gawdy, guilded stage', is a self-conscious exercise on a Jonsonian model imitated also by Carew and Randolph. Another is a free translation from Lucretius beginning 'Greate mother of Eneas and of love'. A diatribe in heroic couplets beginning 'What vaine unnecessary things are men' adopts a persona like that of *Artemisa to Cloe*, but no hint of it survives in the poem as printed. Another fragment mysteriously titled 'Sab: Lost' appears to celebrate the same kind of superhuman beauty as ''Twas a dispute'.

> Shee yeilds, she yeilds, Pale Envy said Amen
> The first of woemen to the Last of men,
> Just soe those fraller beings Angells fell
> Ther's no mid way (it seemes) twix't heav'n and hell,
> Was it your end in making her, to show
> Things must bee rais'd soe high to fall soe low?
> Since her nor Angells their owne worth secures
> Looke to it gods! the next turne must bee yours
> You who in careles scorne Laught att the wayes
> Of Humble Love and call'd 'em rude Essayes
> Could you submitt to Lett this Heavy thing,
> Artless and wittless, noe way meritting
>
> (Walker, 26)

David Vieth spreads the holograph poems over many years. The panegyric he prints as if it were the first thing Rochester ever wrote, in the section of his edition called 'Prentice Work' with putative dating between 1665 and 1671; 'Att last you'l force mee' appears later in the same section; three others he ascribes to 'Early Maturity 1672–1673', and four to 'Tragic Maturity 1674–1675', and one he places in the last section, under the rubric 'Disillusionment and Death 1676–1680', dating it 1679. Such a broad scatter of dates could make sense only if, say, these scraps of paper had been found among the poet's effects years after they had been written, which is just possible. The holograph texts reveal that Rochester is an earnest poet, vividly mindful of the literary traditions in which he is writing; what history tells us is that no courtier could be seen to be so earnest. Other such disregarded scraps of paper must have found their way via the poet's valet or laundress to the Grub Street miscellany makers.

One of the two poems that we know from other sources appears in the holograph as:

> Att Last you'l force mee to confess
> You need noe arts to vanquish
> Such charmes from Nature you posses
> 'Twere dullness, nott to Languish;
> Yett spare A heart you may surprize
> And give my Tongue the glory
> To scorne, while my unfaithfull eyes
> Betray a kinder story.

(Walker, 22)

These eight lines were published in 1676 in *A New Collection of the Choicest Songs* as the end of another of Rochester's songs in four quatrains beginning 'While on those lovely looks I gaze'. As all six quatrains share the alternating masculine–feminine rhyme structure, the conflation may represent the completion of a scheme of which the eight lines in the holograph are but a part. However, a version of the eight lines in the holograph was printed as a separate poem in *Examen Poeticum* in 1693, as 'Another Song in Imitation of Sir *John Eaton*'s Songs'.

> Too late, alas! I must confess
> You need no *Arts* to move me:
> Such Charms by Nature you posses,
> 'Twere madness not to love you.
>
> Then spare a Heart you may surprise,
> And give my Tongue the Glory
> To boast, tho' my unfaithful Eyes
> Betray a kinder Story.

(Walker, 22)

Such instability is typical of texts authored by the Restoration court wits, who began – or had to appear to begin – by improvising on an idea or a form, in this case the iambic tetrameter quatrain, with alternate rhymes alternately masculine and feminine. The likeliest basis for such composition is a pre-existing song which is to be dittied, that is, supplied with new words to be sung to its existing tune. Rochester may have extemporized in company, and later endeavoured to recall some of the quatrains, or he may have contributed quatrains to someone else's version, or he may have had his work edited or improved by a senior wit. In any case it was the pastime that counted. Any courtier who became known to labour over his verse could expect to be ridiculed out of hand.

Another of the poems in Rochester's holograph has survived in very different form. The holograph reads:

> perfect
> How ~~happy~~ Cloris, and how free
>   Would these enjoyments prouve,
> But you with formall jealousy
>   Are still tormenting Love.
>
> Lett us (since witt instructs us how)
>   Raise pleasure to the topp
> If Rivall bottle you'l allow
>   I'le suffer rivall fopp.
>   — ooo —
>
> Ther's not a brisk insipid sparke
>   That flutter in the Towne
> But with your wanton eyes you marke
>   Him out to be your owne.
>
> You never thinke it worth your care
>   How empty nor how dull
> The heads of your admirers are
>   purse
>   Soe that their backs bee full.
>
> All this you freely may confess
>   Yett wee'l not disagree
> For did you love your pleasures less
>   You were not fitt for mee.
>
> Whilst I my passion to persue
>   Am whole nights taking in
>   Lusty juice of
> The ~~juice of Lusty~~ grapes, take you
>   The juice of Lusty Men –
>   — ooo —
>
> Upraide mee not that I designe
>   Tricks to delude your charmes
> When running after mirth and wine
>   I leave your Longing Armes.

> For wine (whose power alone can raise
> Our thoughts soe farr above)
> Affords Idea's fitt to praise
> What wee thinke fitt to Love.[3]

In *Poems on Several Occasions by the Right Honourable, the E. of R*—— (1680) this song was published with substantive variants and without the last two stanzas; a quite different version had appeared four years earlier in *A New Collection of the Choicest Songs*, with the second last stanza, though not the last, plus another, completely new stanza inserted after the second, which can be found in a manuscript copy of the same version in a Harvard manuscript as well as in Tonson's edition of 1691. All these versions may be in some measure due to Rochester; of them the best, in the sense that it is the clearest in sense and most decided in tone, is the one that appears in the worst edition, namely 1680. What the holograph would seem to represent is Rochester's working on an early version of the song of which he would later remember the most trenchant stanzas, which change very little in the several versions, while he reinvented the forgettable ones. We shall never know whether Rochester would have supplied a written copy of such a ballad for his boon companions to sing from, or whether he would have intoned it himself, as if extemporizing, to riotous acclaim.

Songs are written, not in order to entice ladies to one's bed or to drive them out of it, but to be sung. Singing is the boon companion of drinking. Hard drinking had been an integral part of Cavalier culture ever since supporters of the exiled King had gathered to express their loyalty by the drinking of toasts. At the Restoration court drink provided the stimulus that overthrew protocol and produced unforgettable episodes of misrule, which the King appeared to need as much any of his courtiers. Though anacreontic songs must appear to have arisen spontaneously during idle hours or bouts of drinking, and were often dittied to old tunes that had their own associations, they were based on distinct literary models. One of the most popular of these was Anakreonta 19, versions of which can be found in dozens of seventeenth-century commonplace books and miscellanies; those who did not know the original in Greek would have known Cowley's rather verbose version in ten doggerel couplets.

> The thirsty Earth soaks up the Rain,
> And drinks, and gapes for drink again.
> The Plants suck in the earth and are
> With constant drinking fresh and fair. (etc.)

Scholars are divided as to whether this version is by Rochester:

> The Heaven drinks each day a cup,
> No wonder Atlas holds her up.
> The trees suck up the earth and ground,
> And in their brown boles drink around.
> The Sea too, whom the salt makes dry,
> His greedy thirst to satisfy,
> Ten thousand rivers drinks and then
> He's drunk and spews them up again.
> The Sun (and who so right as he)
> Sits up all night to drink the sea.
> The Moon quaffs up the Sun, her brother,
> And wishes she could tope another.
> Everything fuddles, then that I,
> Is't any reason should be dry?
> Well, I'll be content to thirst,
> But too much drink shall make me first.

> (Walker, 127)

Though this poem is attributed to Rochester in two contemporary manuscripts, and in a publication of 1707, two of the most authoritative editors of Rochester, Vivian de Sola Pinto and David Vieth, refuse to include it in the canon. Vieth's reasons for excluding it are 'the poem's clumsy syntax and imprecise diction and meaning'. The poem is actually better than Vieth thinks. What it sets out to do is to burlesque the commonplaces of the anacreontic drinking song by investing them with references so vividly anatomical that they become cannibalistically grotesque. Cowley's attempt, published in 1656, was bound to incur the riotous contempt of the drinking classes. It is typical of Rochester's imagination when under strong stimulus that he pushes the feebler conceits of the original inside out, partly to show their fatuity, at the same time providing an object lesson in the correct use of the hudibrastic couplet as a burlesque metre. Even so, he is more perceptive than Cowley; trees do drink hugely, thousands of gallons a day, through their boles, as he says; he adds the notion of the sea's salt and of spewing as a result of drinking, not so much as hinted at in Cowley's more decorous version. The Sun is personalized as a toper who sits up all night to drink, as Charles was reputed to do upon occasion; a glance at the Sun King's divine right fizzes past as the imagery collapses in a drunken muddle, for which Cowley is to blame, having repeated the original Greek nonsensicality about the moon and stars drinking up the sun. The following sentence too is turned inside out, as the poet makes his final point that drinking to excess causes dehydration as well as nausea. Rochester's is heroic drinking of strong liquor; Cowley might as well be sipping well-water.

Rochester's drinking companions were well able to appreciate the drubbing that he dealt Cowley, as well as the extravagance of the opening personification of Heaven as a tipsy drab supported by her pimp. Still, we cannot be sure that these eight couplets are all by Rochester; some of the men who appreciated them were also capable of writing them. Various versions of Anakreonta 19 were sung in Cavalier drinking clubs as rounds; there is nothing easier or more inevitable than the insertion of saltier words as a round continues, the best versions being accepted as such by common consent. Rochester was acknowledged by his fellows as the readiest and most outrageous but not the only wit. He needed the stimulus of competition with men whose taste and intelligence he respected as much as he needed the alcohol that fuelled their frolicking. Even so, the most spontaneous-seeming drinking song can turn out to be a self-conscious literary exercise: when Rochester warbled

> Vulcan contrive me such a cup
> As Nestor used of old;
> Show all thy skill to trim it up,
> Damask it round with gold...

(Walker, 27, ll. 1–4)

he was probably imitating Ronsard's translation of two of the Anakreonta as a single poem beginning, 'Vulcan! en faveur de moi' or some imitation of it.

Besides drinking songs, a court wit was expected to provide pungent epigrams, impromptus, *bouts rimés*, squibs and lampoons upon demand. So many of these were fathered on Rochester that it is now impossible for scholars to agree which are his. Many of them are simply *jeux d'esprit*, which deploy obscenity for fun, but sex is seldom the real subject matter of Restoration lampoon. In the court milieu of the 1770s obscene fiction was driven by faction, and faction requires a measure of collectivity. A ballad like 'Signor Dildo', accepted by all his modern editors as by Rochester, is typically accretive; its quatrains appear in different order in different sources without agreement as to the total number and with many and considerable variants. While Rochester has been declared solely responsible for a poem called 'Signor Dildo', it is beyond human ingenuity to establish which texts or which parts of which texts are his.[4] Because only one of the eight manuscript sources attributes the poem to Dorset and Fleetwood Shepherd, their part in its composition is usually discounted. What ought to be clear is that Rochester cannot be responsible for all the forms that exist; it seems almost as unlikely that he is responsible for all of the thirty-three quatrains, including some that are not only feeble but unfunny, that can be found in the various manuscripts. The poem is first and foremost an attack on Mary of Modena, the Catholic wife of the heir presumptive to the throne. Its appearance at the end of 1673 shortly after her arrival in England marks the beginning of the underground propaganda campaign against the succession, in which Dorset, Shepherd and Rochester were all implicated – and the beginning of the end of Rochester's career as a courtier.

By the time Rochester's reputation as the most devastating wit in Charles's witty entourage was established, he was already disgusted at his own complaisance. He saw himself with bitter clarity as the King's creature, endlessly ready to humiliate himself for the King's amusement, lower than the royal dogs who pissed with impunity against the courtiers' legs. He may even have had opportunity to contrast his own lot with that of Andrew Marvell, to whom the King, having several times delighted in his company, sent the Lord Treasurer to ask 'how his Majesty could serve him'. Marvell replied 'in his usual facetious manner' 'that it was not in his Majesty's power to serve him', rejecting the offer of a place at court and £1,000 that went with it.[5] Disillusionment came to Rochester long before death; some of his most disgusted and despairing poetry was written at the same time as his most buffoonish lampoons. The state papers and treasury books record repeated attempts by Rochester to accumulate the kinds of offices that would free him from the duties of attendance. It took serious illness finally to secure his manumission.

4

The Poet of Love

In October 1671 a little-known bookseller called Hobart Kemp, whose publishing career lasted little more than twelve months, entered a miscellany in the Stationers' Register which appeared the next year under the title *A Collection of Poems, Written upon Several Occasions, by Several Persons*. Different publishers were to republish the collection five times in ensuing years, and it remains a principal source for the work of Etherege and Sedley. In this first edition, the compilation of which can be dated by the inclusion of Etherege's Prologue for the opening of the new Duke's theatre in Dorset Garden soon after 9 November 1671, none of the poems was attributed. The book was printed into two sections, separately paginated; two poems by Rochester, both called 'To Celia', appear towards the end of the second section. In pride of place at the head of the volume is the longest work in it, a translation of Philippe Habert's *Le Temple de la Mort* by the Earl of Mulgrave.

Mulgrave corresponds to the type of 'blockhead' who was ridiculed in 'The Ballers' Life', a drinking song of the young gentlemen who lived for going to balls, included in part 2 of the 1672 *Collection*:

> They have to many hours that employ 'em
>   About Business, Ambition or News,
>   Whilst we that know how to enjoy 'em
> Wish in vain for the time which such blockheads misuse...[1]

Far from following the Ballers' creed – 'We love and we drink till we dye' – Mulgrave was relentlessly pursuing a dual career as a soldier and a politician. Having built himself a formidable military reputation, he seduced one by one the most powerful court ladies, aided in his conquests by an arrogance and detachment that Rochester could never have commanded. No contemporary court satire couples Rochester's name with that of any court lady, while Mulgrave and his 'lobcock tarse' feature in nearly every one.[2] Rochester seems to have been naturally shy and thin-skinned – Nathaniel Lee refers to a hesitation in his speech[3] – but Mulgrave's sallow skin was never seen to flush. Successful though he was in acquiring power through intrigue and manipulation, he envied the court wits the literary success that they seemed hardly to value and set about building himself a reputation as a wit where they would have scorned to seek it, in print. The likeliest source of Kemp's copies – and the money to publish them with Mulgrave's own poem in pride of place – was Mulgrave. He was to repeat the strategy at regular intervals all his life, as well as paying other poets to praise him and collaborating with Dryden in reviling the wits who, so far from acknowledging him as one of them, persisted in lampooning him without mercy. Mulgrave was a dangerous and experienced duellist who challenged Rochester at least twice. As no duel between them ever took place he had to content himself with murdering Rochester's reputation by branding him a coward. The enmity between the two men was constitutional; Mulgrave was everything Rochester despised, heavy, artless, witless, calculating, self-obsessed, ill-natured, arrogant and cruel.

It is extremely unlikely that Rochester was directly involved in the appearance of his work in print in 1672. As he was to say of himself a few years later:

> I loathe the rabble, 'tis enough for me
> If Sedley, Shadwell, Shepherd, Wycherley,
> Godolphin, Butler, Buckhurst, Buckingham,
> And some few more, whom I omit to name,
> Approve my sense: I count their censure fame.
>
> (Walker, 102, ll. 120–5)

What these lines tell us is that Rochester did publish his work, in the sense that he had copies made to give to the men whose judgement he valued. Such manuscript publishing often led to printing, because the secretaries and amanuenses who actually made the copies knew that booksellers were desperate to get their hands on poems that were being discussed among the court wits and would pay handsomely for them. Most noble authors made the best of the situation by enduring an appearance in print but not acknowledging it. Rochester may not even have known of the printing of two of his poems in 1672; he never claimed them and they were not to be identified as his work until Jacob Tonson brought out the first authorized edition of Rochester's work in 1691, when they appeared in significantly variant forms. These are the last six lines 'To Celia' of the 1672 printing, as if emended for 1691 where the poem is shorn of ten lines and bears a new title, 'The Discovery'.

<pre>
                       design'd
        But Love has carefully contriv'd for me,
        The last perfection of Misery:
                       the
        For to my State those hopes of Common peace,
                 every wretch enjoys in death
        Which Death affords to every wretch, must cease;
                       attend
        My worst of Fates attends me in my Grave,
        Since, dying, I must be no more your Slave.¹
</pre>

There is every possibility that neither form represents the author's final intention; indeed, the author may never have formed a final intention. It would be wrong, however, to conclude from such an example that Rochester was not interested in matters of style. Rather, he was prevented both by his social position and his own attitude from concerning himself with the establishment of a brand-name product.

The firmness of the heroic couplets of the poem 'To Celia' is not what we would expect from journeyman work. The speaker in these amorous addresses assumes the conventional posture of the enslaved and unrequited lover, only to exaggerate it by subtle shifts until the lady's cruelty appears overdone and the lover's submission no less so. Because of their implied emotional context Keith Walker associates with these two a masterful fragment that survives in Rochester's holograph, beginning:

> Could I but make my wishes insolent
> And force some image of a false content!
> But they like mee bashfull and humble growne
> Hover att distance about Beautyes throne
> There worship and admire and then they die
> Dareing noe more Lay Hold of her than I.
>
> (Walker, 17, ll. 1–6)

Rochester's governing idea, of the man unmanned by love, is a commonplace, but the sudden irruption of the urge to lay hold of the *woman* into the language of extreme deference offered to the *lady* brings home with a bump the awareness of infatuation as dying in its own too-much. This is a lover who knows what it is to take a woman, contemplating the one woman he can never take, even if she wants him to, because of the intensity of his own emotion. Such sophistication in understanding the velleities of sexual feeling is what the Restoration love lyric strove to demonstrate. The source of all was Ovid, not the Ovid that Rochester had studied at Burford but the forbidden *Amores*. Rochester and his peers knew well that Marlowe had translated the *Amores*, and that his translations, their first English printing having been burnt by order of the bishops, were available only in surreptitious Dutch editions. They knew too that the complex ironies and understatements of the *Amores* underlay the elegies of John Donne. In the *Amores* they found compressed expression of the complex feelings of an intelligent man alternately exalted and degraded by his own sexual obsession, which he both celebrates and derides. The drama in the *Amores* is not played out between a man and his beloved but between a man and his sexuality; the putative hearer/reader is not the lady but a man like himself. It seems likely that Rochester sat down to translate *Amores* 2:9 fairly early in his career. One coincidence suggests that he might have had Marlowe's translation before him. Ovid's Latin reads:

> O numquam pro re satis indignande Cupido,
> o in corde meo desidiose puer –
> quid me, qui miles numquam tua signa reliqui,
> laedis, et in castris vulneror ipse meis?

Marlowe translates:

> O Cupid, that dost never cease thy smart,
> O boy, that liest so slothful in my heart,
> Why me that always was thy soldier found,
> Dost harm, and in thy tents why dost me wound?[5]

In three of the seven manuscripts and in four printings of the 1680s Rochester follows Marlowe's mistake of translating 'thy' for 'my' in the fourth line:

O Love, how cold and slow to take my part!
Thou idle wanderer about my heart,
Why thy old faithful soldier wilt thou see
Oppressed in thy own tents? They murder me.

(Walker, 49, ll. 1–4)

Vieth, following modern practice, divides the elegy into two separate poems as neither Marlowe nor Rochester does. As Marlowe's editor Roma Gill notices, it was Marlowe's choice that established the heroic couplet as the accepted equivalent of Ovid's elegiac metre. There can be no doubting that Rochester's translation pays homage to Marlowe as the trailblazer of a libertine tradition.

The *Amores* pervades Rochester's thought; his Corinna, whether rambling in St James's Park or pawning her Mantua gown for half a crown, is recognizably Ovid's Corinna. Rochester would have found the authority for treating the theme of sexual impotence in *Amores* 3:7, but 'The Imperfect Enjoyment' demonstrates the extent to which he uses the classical precedent to explore a different situation and sensibility. Ovid's persona is unable to produce an erection: Rochester's ejaculates prematurely, as his mistress Corinna guides his member with her hand. Ovid's lover fails, not with his lady love Corinna, who has been known to ask and get nine episodes of intromission in a night, but with a stranger. Rochester's lover is where he has always longed to be. He puts to his sexuality a question Ovid would not have thought to ask.

Through what mistaken magic dost thou prove
So true to lewdness, so untrue to love?

(Walker, 31, ll. 48–9)

For Rochester it is *caritas* that dignifies *amor*. It is the Christian view that where *agape* or *caritas* meets *eros* or *amor* there God is. In *Artemisa to Cloe*, one of his most influential poems, twice printed in broadside in 1679 and surviving in more than twenty manuscript copies, the female poet Artemisa explains the place of love in Rochester's teleology:

Love, the most generous passion of the mind,
The softest refuge innocence can find,
The safe director of unguided youth,
Fraught with kind wishes and secured by truth,

41

> That cordial drop heaven in our cup has thrown
> To make the nauseous draught of life go down...
>
> (Walker, 84, ll. 40–5)

The interdependence of the repellent and the adorable creates the ironic tension in all Rochester's best sex poetry from the song of 'A Young Lady to her Ancient Lover' to 'A Ramble in St James's Park'. Rochester's praise of love, imitated so often as to become a minor genre in itself, is Ovidian in feeling but has no Ovidian precedent, transformed as it is by Rochester's Christian moral sensibility. Rochester knew that mortal creatures are not organized for bliss, and that true love is known by increase not of pleasure but of pain:

> An age in her embraces passed
>   Would seem a winter's day,
> Where life and light with envious haste
>   Are torn and snatched away.
>
> But oh, how slowly minutes roll
>   When absent from her eyes
> That feed my love, which is my soul.
>   It languishes and dies,
>
> For then no more a soul but shade,
>   It mournfully does move;
> And haunts my breast, by absence made
>   The living tomb of love.
>
> You wiser men despise me not,
>   Whose love-sick fancy raves
> On shades of souls, and heaven knows what:
>   Short ages live in graves.
>
> Whene'er those wounding eyes, so full
>   Of sweetness you did see,
> Had you not been profoundly dull,
>   You had gone mad like me.
>
> Nor censure us you who perceive
>   My best beloved and me
> Sigh and lament, complain and grieve.
>   You think we disagree.
>
> Alas! 'tis sacred jealousy,
>   Love raised to an extreme,
> The only proof 'twixt her and me
>   We love and do not dream.

Fantastic fancies fondly move
And frail joys believe,
Taking false pleasures for true love,
But pain can ne'er deceive.

Kind jealous doubts, tormenting fears,
And anxious cares, when past,
Prove our hearts' treasure fixed and dear,
And make us blest at last.

(Walker, 29–30)

This poem was not published until Tonson collected it in 1691 and it survives in no manuscript. The paradox, that though fools cannot love love makes fools of men of wit, is fundamental to Rochester's thought but both the rapture and the pain of 'An age in her embraces past' would have been familiar to other gentleman wits. Among the versicles in the pocket-sized commonplace book, bound in black leather and clasped with silver, found on Buckingham at his death in 1687, we may read:

No! in the golden age there was no love
The hony which on every tree did grow
And Rivers, which with milk did flow
With that to boot, would bitter prove.
With famine, plagues & war the God came in
The Tyrant Beauty, and vsurper Iove
She vpon earth, & hee above
Did both theyr raignes at once begin.[6]

The thought in Rochester's poem is vastly more complex. The lover is made immortal by love, which like God (who is love) creates and maintains his soul. When love is absent his soul becomes a shade, as it were, an unredeemed pre-Christian soul condemned for eternity to exist in a realm outside heaven. The fourth stanza raves and the fifth pulls the sense together, with the typically Rochesterian thought that anyone who did not see the celestial power in his mistress's face would have to be 'profoundly dull'. According to Rochester 'The poet's talent is to love and rail'; railing is a part of love because love goads to painful madness. The seventh stanza bears marks of Rochester's reading of Donne. The argument of the last stanza, that love's suffering proves love true and earns heaven, displays as much awareness of the dynamic of redemption as it does of the workings of passion.

Rochester's interrogation of his own sexuality reached its apogee in 'A Ramble in St James's Park' which was circulating in manuscript by March 1673. The poem creates St James's Park, known to all to be a place of promiscuous sexual encounter, as a phallic landscape sollipsistically constructed in the imagination of the questing male, who interprets every event within it as an analogue of erection and orgasm. Into this organ concerto steps Corinna, the ever-available female to the poet's persona only unavailable. He watches as she is courted like a bitch in heat by three contemptible male figures, all of whom have a better prospect of success than he. He then recounts the history of his relationship with her, which begins with his humiliating consent to be one of her many lovers only to be ridiculed for his inadequacies and ultimately rejected. The poem ends with his curse, condemning her to insatiable nymphomania and a lifetime of persecution by him, until she is

> Loathed and despised, kicked out of town
> Into some dirty hole alone,
> To chew the cud of misery,
> And know she owes it all to me.
>   And may no woman better thrive
>   Who dares profane the cunt I swive.
>
> (Walker, 68, ll. 161–6)

The subject of this poem is not Corinna but the vengeful, inadequate, ludicrous and dangerous figure of the rejected male. Corinna is glimpsed from a distance by a previously successful but now rejected lover much as the beloved is in Catullus LI, 'Ille mi par esse deo videtur'. Though Corinna dances through her rejected lover's obsessional torment like the phantom of the *belle dame sans merci*, Rochester's pity is not for her victim but for her. His evocation of the ultimate fate of the public beauty is tragic. Rochester, inasmuch as he was a public performer caressed by the undiscerning, was no better than she and could expect a similar fate. As he explained in *A Satire against Mankind*:

> And wit was his vain frivolous pretence,
> Of pleasing others at his own expense,
> For wits are treated just like common whores:
> First they're enjoyed, and then kicked out of doors.
>
> (Walker, 92, ll. 37–8)

5

The Female Impersonator

Nowadays few male poets would dare to adopt a female voice, but in the seventeenth century poets as apparently macho as Ben Jonson, who had killed a man, did not shrink from speaking as women of women's affairs. Marvell could be a nymph upon occasion. Rochester had no hesitation in writing in a female voice; indeed, adopting a female persona seems to have permitted a kind of paradoxicality in his thinking that was not accessible to masculine authority. The classical precedent was to be found in the *Heroides*, Ovid's impersonation of the most famous heroines of antiquity, although every dramatist of every age has written for heroic female characters.

In 1673 Rochester impersonated a real woman in order to chastise a fellow-courtier. Negotiations for the marriage of Henrietta Maria Price, one of Queen Catherine's Maids of Honour, had been jeopardized by the boasting of Lord Chesterfield, erstwhile Chamberlain to the Queen, that the lady was in love with him. Miss Price could not afford to antagonize so powerful a personage but she had somehow to stop his mouth. Rochester came to the rescue by penning a note for her to include with the rich present of a pair of Italian gloves:

> My Lord –
> These are the gloves that I did mention
> Last night and 'twas with the intention
> That you should give me thanks and wear them,
> For I most willingly can spare them.

Having impersonated the embarrassed young woman, it was easy to switch to impersonating the presumptuous grandee himself.

> When you this packet first do see,
> 'Damn me,' cry you, 'she has writ to me;
> I'd better be at Bretby still
> Than troubled with love against my will.
> Besides, this is not all my sorrow:
> She's writ today, she'll come tomorrow.'

Chesterfield took the present and the point that it was prompted by

> neither love nor passion
> But only for your recreation.
>
> (Walker, 61–2, ll. 1–4, 5–10, 15–16)

Miss Price's marriage with his kinsman Alexander Stanhope went ahead. Chesterfield copied the poem into his letter-book and, we may hope, behaved with more circumspection thereafter.

Rochester was unusually aware that for his female contemporaries sex was a blood-sport. Daphne, in the eclogue 'A Dialogue between Strephon and Daphne', probably the first of his female impersonations, in love with Strephon who is tired of her, woos him in vain. He crushes her with the observation that 'Change has greater charms than you'. Daphne learns from this to follow the Rochesterian principle:

> Womankind more joy discovers
> Making fools than keeping lovers.
>
> (Walker, 14, ll. 71–2)

The speaker of the song 'Injurious charmer of my vanquished heart' from *Valentinian* is a nymph who regrets the easiness with which she entered into intimacy. She asks her lover to 'invent some gentle way to let [her] go'

> For what with joy thou didst obtain,
> And I with more did give,
> In time will make thee false and vain,
> And me unfit to live.
>
> (Walker, 28, ll. 5–8)

By no means all of Rochester's female selves are victims; some are aggressors. In the song 'To her Ancient Lover' a very young Lady proposes to take very un-ladylike liberties:

> On thy withered lips and dry,
> Which like barren furrows lie,
> Brooding kisses I will pour,
> Shall thy youthful heat restore
>
> .   .   .   .   .
>
> Thy nobler part, which but to name
> In our sex would be counted shame,
> By age's frozen grasp possessed,
> From his ice shall be released:
> And soothed by my reviving hand
> In former warmth and vigour stand...
>
> (Walker, 33, ll. 7–10, 13–20)

Rochester's 'Platonic Lady' is another who actively seeks her own pleasure. The poem is a variation on the pseudo-Petronian theme *Foeda est in coitu et brevis voluptas* with its implied rejection of vulgar notions of sexual prowess.

> I love a youth will give me leave
> His body in my arms to wreathe,
> To press him gently and to kiss...
>
> .   .   .   .   .
>
> I'd give him liberty to toy
> And play with me and count it joy.
> Our freedom should be full complete
> And nothing wanting but the feat.
>
> (Walker, 24, ll. 13–15, 19–22)

Stranger, and undeniably authentic, are the fifty-five lines of dramatic monologue in Rochester's holograph, that begin

> What vaine unnecessary things are men
> How well we do with out 'em, tell me then
> Whence comes that meane submissivness wee finde
> This ill bred age has wrought on womankinde...
>
> (Walker, 90, ll. 1–4)

In the late 1670s occurred a set of circumstances that produced the literary figure of 'Ephelia', a jilted Maid of Honour, who may or may not have had an actual historic counterpart. The court wits went into battle for her against their sworn enemy Mulgrave; first Etherege penned an epistle from Ephelia to her unconstant gallant or 'Bajazet', then Rochester weighed in with Bajazet's answer or *A Very Heroical Epistle from My Lord All-Pride to Dol-Common*:

Madam,
If you're deceived, it is not by my cheat,
For all disguises are below the great.
What man or woman upon earth can say
I ever used 'em well above a day?
How is it then that I inconstant am?
He changes not who always is the same.
In my dear self I centre everything,
My servants, friends, my mistress and my King,
Nay, heaven and earth to that one point I bring.

(Walker, 112, ll. 1–9)

There is little doubt that while Rochester disappointed his mother, his wife, his mistress and his daughters, he was obsessed and fascinated by women. It is not surprising that the sensitive son of a woman like Anne Rochester should be aware of his spiritual self as female. This was one of the many things about Rochester that Burnet could not understand. Most of Rochester's utterance as reported in *Some Passages in the Life and Death of the Right Honourable John Earl of Rochester* is uncomprehending paraphrase, but occasionally Rochester's frame of reference shows through: 'But for the next state', Burnet wrote, 'he thought it more likely that the soul began anew, and that her sense of what she had done in this body, lying in the figures that are made in the Brain, as soon as she dislodged, all these perished'. Nowhere else does Burnet write of the soul as female. The dying Rochester is supposed to have asked:

> What a pox have the Women to do with the Muses? I grant you the Poets call the nine Muses by the names of Women, but why so? not because the Sex has anything to do with Poetry, but because in the Sex they're much fitter for prostitution.[1]

These words are usually understood to reflect on women; they actually reflect on poetry. Rochester had explained the parallel before, in the epilogue he wrote for Charles Davenant's play, *Circe*:

> Poets and women have an equal right
> To hate the dull who, dead to all delight,
> Feel pain alone and have no joy but spite...
>
> .   .   .   .   .   .
>
> Since therefore to the women it appears
> That all these enemies of wit are theirs,
> Our poet the dull herd no longer fears.

(Walker, 58, ll. 10–12, 17–19)

As Artemis sprang fully armed from the head of Zeus, Rochester brought forth Artemisa, virgin poet and wit. The verse epistle Rochester wrote in her persona, *Artemisa to Cloe*, was first printed as a broadside in 1679. It seems that 1679 was the year of the female poet: both *Ephelia to Bajazet* and Rochester's 'Very Heroicall Epistle in Answer' as well as the first issue of *Female Poems on Several Occasions by Ephelia* appeared that year. Rochester's Artemisa is better known than any of these; *Female Poems on Several Occasions* did not sell; it was reissued in 1682 plumped out with an added section of poems associated with Rochester, whereas the broadside of *Artemisa to Cloe* sold out and was reprinted in the same year. A better indication of the intense interest Rochester's poem aroused is that it is to be found in no fewer than twenty-three contemporary manuscripts (Walker, 190–1). By 1700 it had appeared in six further printings. Quotations from it can be found embedded in all kinds of writing.

What Artemisa writes to Cloe is a Horatian epistle in a low and familiar style. She disparages herself, as Horace does, by invoking an implicit standard of right feeling and common sense which she herself cannot claim to have attained. Having curtsied to the convention that she should write only in response to a command, she rattles on into a comparison of versifying with such masculine pastimes as riding astride and fighting, only to pitch poetry rather higher, invoking the subliminal image of Pegasus in her reference to the 'lofty flights of dangerous poetry'. The image gallops on into a pathless stormy world which becomes an ocean where poet privateers dare destruction for the bays.

> When I reflect on this, I straight grow wise
> And my own self thus gravely I advise,
> 'Dear Artemisa, poetry's a snare.
> Bedlam has many mansions – have a care.
> Your Muse diverts you, makes the reader sad;
> You fancy you're inspired, he thinks you mad...
>
> (Walker, 83, ll. 14–19)

Rochester, like Artemisa, was a poet against his better judgement. His itch to show off plus his verbal incontinence pushed him time and again into catastrophic indiscretions which brought swift and condign punishment in their train. When it came to defending himself he had no remedy but Jonson's:

> Thou callst me poet, as a term of shame:
> But I have my revenge made, in thy name.[2]

So he might have considered himself revenged against Mulgrave in lampooning him as 'Lord All-Pride'.

Artemisa knows that

> Whore is scarce a more reproachful name
> Than Poetesse:

> (Walker, 83, ll. 26–7)

but 'arrant woman' as she is, she cannot cure her itch to write. Though Artemisa expresses the problem in terms of gender, gender was not the crucial factor. The imputation of immodesty, of seeking praise by a promiscuous display of wit, could have been levelled at Rochester himself. If Rochester had been able to rein in his wit he might have become a rich and powerful man, and he could have been a great poet if his rank had not impeded his full development as effectively as Artemisa's sex would impede hers. He could not sit and toil over his lines as Dryden or Cowley might do. He might like nothing better than showing in a brilliant couplet or two what was wrong with both of them, but he was not permitted to care what became of his efforts. He accepted contributions and collaboration from less gifted men, and never troubled himself to record an authorized version of even his most deeply felt poetry.

The break in the regularity of the couplets between lines 27 and 28 of *Artemisa to Cloe*, and the slightly awkward bridging passage that follows before the poem as it were restarts at line 32, could be a sign that the poem was begun as part of an interchange to which Cloe too would contribute, rather in the manner of the interchanges between Ephelia and Bajazet. In a *Miscellany* of 1720 appears a fragment called 'Cloe to Artemisa':

> While vulgar souls their vulgar love pursue,
> And in the common way themselves undo;
> Impairing health and fame and risking life,
> To be a mistress, or, what's worse, a wife:
> We whom a nicer taste has raised above
> The dangerous follies of such slavish love,
> Despise the sex, and in ourselves we find
> Pleasures for their gross senses too refined...[3]

In the poem which appears next in the miscellany, 'The Return', the lines in praise of love from *Artemisa to Cloe* are quoted and credited to 'Bion', the poetic sobriquet that the poetaster Robert Wolseley used for Rochester.[4] In Bodleian MS Don b. 8, the most authoritative source for the *Artemisa to Cloe*, a note opposite line 251 says: 'This poeme is supposed to bee made by the Earle of Rochester, or Mr Wolseley.' The insertion of the note at one of the several passages in the poem where the energy seems to flag might provide a clue to some of the structural weaknesses that cause the taut thread of Artemisa's thought to slacken and even to sag into lampoon (e.g. ll. 66–72). 'The lyric poet with the sevenfold skull' may have been involved in the original project and interpolated contributions of his own, supplying duller connective tissue for brilliant fragments by Rochester.[5]

Artemisa begins her letter *in propria persona*, then, as a mirror within a mirror, introduces the fine lady to whom was known 'Every one's fault and merit but her own', who in turn introduces Corinna.

> That wretched thing Corinna who had run
> Through all the several ways of being undone,
> Cozened at first by love, and living then
> By turning the too dear bought trick on men.
>
> .   .   .   .
>
> Courted, admired, loved, with presents fed,
> Youth in her looks and pleasure in her bed,
> Till Fate or her ill angel thought it fit
> To make her dote upon a man of wit,
> Who found 'twas dull to love above a day,
> Made his ill-natured jest and went away.
> Now scorned by all, forsaken and oppressed,
> She's a memento mori to the rest;
> Diseased, decayed, to take up half a crown
> Must mortgage her long scarf and mantua gown.
> Poor creature who, unheard of, as a fly
> In some dark hole must all the winter lie,
> That for one month she tawdry may appear.
>
> (Walker, 88, ll. 189–92, 195–208)

The scorn here is the fine lady's, but the pity comes from Rochester. This vignette is truer to the actual circumstances of a woman of wit like Aphra Behn, whom Rochester certainly knew and may have collaborated with, than any suffragette version of her as a woman of independent means or late twentieth-century triumphalist vision of her as a feisty feminist bisexual.

In 1676 Rochester created a heroine of the feistiest and most feminist, namely Amocoa, Empress of China, in the scene that he wrote for Sir Robert Howard's 'Conquest of China by the Tartars', probably simply to oblige the man who in 1644 had rescued the poet's father when he was wounded and taken prisoner at Cropredy Bridge. Howard, who was appointed auditor of the Exchequer in 1677, did not find the time to finish his play. Rochester's contribution, which survives in two manuscripts, can be authenticated from Howard's letter to the poet, dated 7 April 1676.[6]

Amocoa, who appears on stage at the head of an army, rejects any suggestion that she is unfit for command:

> Woman is born
> With equal thirst of honour and of fame,
> But treacherous man misguides her in her aim,
> Makes her believe that all her glories lie
> In dull obedience, truth and modesty,
> That to be beautiful is to be brave,
> And calls her conqueror when she's most his slave,
> Forbidding her those noble paths to tread
> Which through bold daring deeds to glory lead,
> With the poor hypocritical pretence
> That woman's merit is her innocence,
> Who treacherously advised retaining thus
> The sole ambition to be virtuous
> Thinks 'tis enough if she's not infamous.

(Ellis, 184, ll. 9–22)

Amocoa announces the dawn of a new era in which

> Woman henceforth by [her] example taught
> To vaster heights of virtue shall be wrought.
> Trained up in war and arts she shall despise
> The mean pretended conquests of her eyes,
> Nor be contented with the low applause
> Left to her sex by man's tyrannic laws.

(Ellis, 185, ll. 25–30)

When she selects Hyachian for her general, passing over Lycungus, he rails against her:

> Who in the dumb greensickness of her mind
> Still hungers for the trash of all mankind.
> Not an insipid fop on earth does move
> For whom some woman does not die in love.
>
> (Ellis, 187, ll. 122-5)

So are we brought back via Artemisa's commonplace to the chagrin of the rejected wit in St James's Park.

6

The Poet in the Theatre

In Rochester's London courtiers thronged to the theatre and, as the most conspicuous members of the audience and part of the spectacle, led the applause or derision. Occasionally a court wit would expose himself to the supreme risk of writing for the stage. In 1664 Sir George Etherege had a success with *The Comical Revenge, or Love in a Tub*, which when it was published was dedicated to Lord Buckhurst; this success was repeated in 1667 with *She would if she could*. In 1668 Sir Charles Sedley had his greatest success with *The Mulberry Garden*. In 1776 Etherege produced his masterpiece, *The Man of Mode or Sir Fopling Flutter*, in which the character Dorimant was said to be modelled on Rochester, which is probably as true as such assertions ever are.

Rochester's poetic imagination was essentially dramatic; even his most lyrical poems presuppose not only a speaker but a situation. The longer poems in heroic couplets are often theatrical, presenting one scene after another, or scenes within scenes. Rochester's voices are always colloquial, and often so sharply individual that an entire personality can be extrapolated from an idiom. As early as 1672 Dryden, reading Rochester's self-consciously literary couplets in *A Collection of Poems, Written upon Several Occasions, by Several Persons* knew that they crackled with nervous energy. Not long afterwards he sought Rochester's help with his new comedy, *Marriage A-la-Mode*, which took the boards in March 1673. When the play was subsequently published, it was dedicated to Rochester. Dryden expressed his relief that Rochester had so far no ambition to write for the theatre.

> I must confess, that I have so much self-interest, as to be content with reading some papers of your verses, without desiring you should proceed to a scene, or play; with the common prudence of those who are worsted in a duel, and declare they are satisfied, when they are first wounded.[1]

54

In the spring of 1673 Rochester wrote a prologue for the second of the performances at court of Elkanah Settle's *Empress of Morocco*. (His enemy Mulgrave wrote the prologue for the first performance.) In 1674 Nathaniel Lee dedicated to Rochester his tragedy *Nero* and Sir Francis Fane his comedy *Love in the Dark*. At the same time he was encouraging Thomas Otway with his heroic tragedy *Don Carlos*, which was played with huge success, and when printed carried Otway's effusive thanks in a preface. Within months Rochester had begun work on his own piece of theatre, an adaptation of John Fletcher's tragedy *Valentinian*. The manuscript of the play in the British Museum gives a cast list that could only have been assembled in the 1675–6 season. Rochester's play must then have been ready for production, but no performance was mounted.

In adapting Fletcher Rochester was following the precedent set by Buckingham, who adapted both *The Chances*, in 1667 or so, and *Philaster*, as *The Restauration, or Right will take place*. Thematically *Valentinian* is related to Rochester's most disastrous satire on the King. In January 1674 the King asked to see a lampoon of Rochester's that he had heard spoken of. The poet plucked a folded paper from his fob; the King took it and read with mounting astonishment and displeasure:

> In the isle of Great Britain long since famous grown
> For breeding the best cunts in Christendom,
> There reigns, and, oh, long may he reign and thrive,
> The easiest King and best bred man alive.
> Him no ambition moves to get renown,
> Like the French fool who wanders up and down,
> Starving his subjects, hazarding his crown.
> Peace is his aim, his gentleness is such,
> And love he loves, for he loves fucking much.
> Nor are his high desires above his strength;
> His sceptre and his prick are of a length...
>
> (Walker, 74, ll. 1–11)

The parallel between penis and prerogative is significant. In court satires sex is the commonest metaphor for politics; here the King's priapism functions as an obscene correlative for arbitrary government. The idea was capable of expansion in all kinds of ways.

Poor prince, thy prick, like thy buffoons at court,
Will govern thee, because it makes thee sport.
'Tis sure the sauciest prick that e'er did swive,
The proudest, peremptoriest prick alive.
Though safety, law, religion, life lay on't,
'Twould break through all to make its way to cunt.

(Walker, 74, ll. 14–19)

Charles could have tolerated the burlesque of his sexual susceptibility, but he was too intelligent not to grasp the underlying condemnation of his personal rule as defying safety, law and religion, even without Rochester's gloss on his own text:

I hate all monarchs and the thrones they sit on,
From the hector of France to the cully of Britain.[2]

(Walker, 75, ll. 32–3)

Written copies being necessarily few, this poem was to become famous in memorial reconstruction, as the vast array of variants in the manuscript record show that it did. Rochester did not wait for the King's wrath to fall but fled the court and went into hiding. Marvell, who teased out every trace of creeping popery and absolutism in merciless but less spectacular poems of his own, recognized that Rochester was 'the best English satirist and had the right veine'. Marvell had been the tutor of the wife of Buckingham, who was his friend and patron as he was Rochester's. When Rochester was appointed to the Lords' committee charged with finding and disciplining all those connected with the publication of Marvell's pamphlet *The Growth of Popery and Arbitrary Government in England. More particularly from the long prorogation of November 1675*, he was probably there as Buckingham's observer. At least since the winter of 1675 when he sat down to write his formal 'Allusion to Horace' Rochester saw himself and was seen as a member of the literary opposition, together with Sedley, Shadwell, Shepherd, Wycherley, Godolphin, Butler, Buckhurst and Buckingham. Marvell and probably by this time Oldham were amongst those whom he chose not to name in a poem the political subtext of which was more perceptible to his contemporaries than it has been to modern editors. As Defoe was quick to realize, Rochester's wit 'made the Court odious to the People, beyond what would have been possible if the press had been open'.[3]

In choosing to work on Fletcher's *Valentinian* during the prorogation Rochester was actually embarking on a collaboration with a dead poet. He made no attempt to make Fletcher's play his own; rather he did as Hamlet does with 'The Mousetrap', simply rearranged the order of scenes and inserted additional dialogue, leaving whole scenes unaltered. Of *Valentinian*'s 2,890 lines, only 1,378 are by Rochester. The new material is mostly in blank verse but, when the speeches rise in rhetorical intensity, they harden into rhyming couplets which close with the genuine Rochesterian snap. Fletcher's *Valentinian* uses the occasion of the rape of Lucina by the monarch to question the limits both of a subject's duty of passive obedience and of royal impunity. Valentinian having violated the chaste wife of his loyal subject Maximus is poisoned by Aecius who has already taken poison himself; Maximus then ascends the throne only to be killed by barbarians loyal to Valentinian's widow Eudoxa. Rochester dispensed with the latter part of the intrigue, ending his play with the murder of the king not by Aecius but by the army loyal to Aecius. The new version is more unified than Fletcher's, more classical than Jacobean, but it is also much more subversive, as the discussions of the subject's duty to the monarch end in insurrection and regicide. Mingling his own voice with Fletcher's was one way Rochester could remind Charles, who had the discrimination to recognize the blank verse of an earlier era, that the struggle against arbitrary power had been going on ever since 'Shakespeare, Fletcher, Jonson ruled the stage'. In case the King should miss the point, Aphra Behn's prologue for the first day's performance underlined it:

> Wit, sacred Wit, is all the bus'ness here;
> Great *Fletcher* and the greater *Rochester*.
> Now name the hardy Man one fault dares find
> In the vast work of two such Heroes joyn'd.[4]

Fletcher's authority was not enough, however, to bring the play onto the stage; Langbaine tells that Fletcher's *The Maid's Tragedy* in which the king who has debauched the hero's wife is killed in revenge 'had still continued on the English stage had not King Charles the Second for particular Reasons forbid its further Appearance during his Reign'.[5] In 1689 Waller altered *The Maid's Tragedy* so that it would be playable; Rochester's alteration can only have made *Valentinian* less playable, especially when the prologue insisted on the parallel with the present:

> For sure no Age was ever known before
> Wanting an *Aecius* and *Lucina* more.

In Fletcher's play, Lucina resists the blandishments both of pandars who promise her empire, and of women who seek to persuade her that she and her husband have nothing to lose and everything to gain by her complaisance, only to be lured to the palace by a ruse and raped by Valentinian. She goes home and, with very little palaver, dies, barely halfway through the play, which then proceeds to examine the options open to Maximus, her wronged husband. Rochester's adaptation opens with twenty-seven new lines in which Lucina's husband exults in the favour shown to his house by three visits from the emperor and his 'gay court'. Aecius answers with a criticism of the monarch:

> Think how he may by the force of worth and virtue
> Maintain the right of his imperial crown,
> Which he neglects for garlands made of roses;
> Whilst in disdain for his ill-guided youth,
> Whole provinces fall off, and scorn to have
> Him for their prince, who is his pleasure's slave.
>
> (Ellis, 103, I. i. 22–7)

Rochester's Valentinian is all too recognizable as the 'easiest king and best bred man alive' who spent on the women who could excite his jaded appetites the money he should have used to reward his loyal servants and fight for the Protestant cause in Europe. Another inserted speech adds to Charles's identikit.

> Yet even his errors have their good effects:
> For the same gentle temper, which inclines
> His mind to softness, does his heart defend
> From savage thoughts of cruelty and blood,
> Which through the streets of Rome in streams did flow
> From hearts of senators under the reigns
> Of our severest war-like Emperors,
> While under this, scarcely one criminal
> Meets the harsh sentence of the dooming law,
> And the whole world, dissolved into a peace,
> Owes its security to this man's pleasures.
>
> (Ellis, 104–5, I. i. 90–100)

Valentinian, who is usually called Caesar, as was Charles in thousands of panegyrical verses, is the king of the Act of Indemnity and Oblivion, bitterly interpreted as indemnity for those who profited in the upheaval of civil war and its aftermath and oblivion for those who endured exile, bereavement and expropriation. 'Softness' is a key concept in Rochester's play, replacing Fletcher's 'woman', meaning susceptibility to pleasure.

Rochester's too is the scene in which Valentinian woos Lucina, praising her love above empire. Lucina's arguments in defence of married chastity, a characteristically Protestant topos, are simpler in tone but no less powerful in effect:

> Fixed in my Maximus breast I lie!
> Torn from that bed, like gathered flowers I die.

> (Ellis, 109, I. i. 266–7)

Only by saying that she will consult the oracles to find out if the gods agree that she should give way to the monarch's advances can Lucina extricate herself from the royal presence without a breach of protocol. Valentinian summons his bawds and talks with Jonsonian plainness to them.

> As ever you do hope to be by me
> Protected in your boundless infamy,
> For dissoluteness cherished, loved and praised,
> On pyramids of your own vices raised,
> Above the reach of law, reproof or shame,
> Assist me now to quench my raging flame.

> (Ellis, 110, I. i. 300–5)

He assures them that all he needs is the love of a good woman.

> Lucina's love my virtue would secure.
> From the contagious charm in vain I fly,
> That seized upon my heart and may defy
> That great preservative, variety!

> (Ellis, 110, I. i. 314–17)

Lucina is then lured to a court that Rochester has transformed with a few deft touches into Whitehall. A wooing madrigal by Rochester is sung and when Lucina declares that she does not understand such things, she is told with a leer that Caesar 'Has the best talent for expounding 'em' and hustled into an inner chamber which closes upon her (Ellis, 144, IV. ii. 116). Dancing-masters appear and practise a new step to the music being played to drown the agonized screams that emerge from the closed inner stage. Then Fletcher's play continues, as Lucina fearlessly denounces Valentinian, takes her leave from her husband forever, and goes home to die. Maximus and Aecius writhe under a subject's duty, their sufferings heightened by a line or two from Rochester: Aecius, the old soldier, warns Maximus:

> However you be tainted, be no traitor.
>
> (Ellis, 156, IV. iii. 292)

His heart aches for the extremity of Maximus' grief

> Which since I cannot like a man redress,
> With tears I must lament it, like a child.
> For when 'tis Caesar does the injury,
> Sorrow is all the remedy I know.
>
> (Ellis, 157, IV. iii. 336–9)

Maximus raves against powers that could ordain that, though guiltless, he is condemned to infamy. His speech is aimed against the contemporary political theory that saw the monarch, no matter how depraved, as God's representative on earth, which Maximus interprets to mean that God must be evil, and so he decides to kill Valentinian, only to come to his senses and pray that he shall not 'fall from truth', that is, commit treason. Act V begins with Aecius' meditation on the dilemma of the loyal subject:

> As well may I kill my offended friend,
> As think to punish my offending prince.
> The laws of friendship we ourselves create,
> And 'tis but simple villainy to break 'em.
> But faith to princes broke is sacrilege,
> An injury to the Gods.
>
> (Ellis, 160, v. i. 4–9)

His soliloquy is interrupted by a courtier to whom he speaks in Rochesterian tones.

> You witty fools are apt to get your heads broke.
> This is no season for buffooning, sirrah.
> Though heretofore I tamely have endured
> Before the Emperor your ridiculous mirth,
> Think not you have a title to be saucy:

> When monkeys grow mischievous, they are whipped,
> Chained up and whipped.
>
> (Ellis, 161, v. i. 36–42)

The next scene is Fletcher's until Valentinian sees Aecius' letter, to which he reacts in true 1670s fashion, by detecting a plot. Fletcher's play resumes as an assassin sent to Aecius commits suicide rather than carry out the royal instructions. Scene V is all Rochester. It opens to show Valentinian on a couch with the eunuch Lycias:

> Oh let me press thy balmy lips all day,
> And bathe my love-scorched soul in thy moist kisses.
> Now by my joys thou art all sweet and soft,
> And thou shalt be the altar of my love
>
> .   .   .   .   .
>
> No god or goddess ever was adored
> With such religion as my love shall be.
> For in these charming raptures of my soul,
> Clasped in thy arms I'll waste myself away, . . .
>
> (Ellis, 176, v. v. 1–14)

In the British Library manuscript of *Valentinian* these lines are so heavily scored out as to be illegible. The king's sodomitical raptures are interrupted by Aecius, who bursts in and scolds him as only a loyal old soldier could. Then, laying his sword at his feet, he invites the king to kill him with his own hand. The king sneers at him to find a hangman or 'beg a milder death among the guards'. Aecius replies:

> Ill-counselled, thankless prince, you did indeed
> Bestow that office on a soldier
> But in the army could you hope to find
> With all your bribes a murderer of Aecius?
>
> (Ellis, 177, v. v. 51–4)

Since only heaven can punish the king, Aecius slaughters his 'base assister', the eunuch in his arms. The king demands a sword to avenge his catamite's death and Aecius, to avoid the heinous sin of treason, runs on it. Valentinian addresses the corpse in terms that reveal the reality that lies behind the rhetoric of absolute power:

> Old Aecius! where is now thy name in war?
> Thy interest with so many conquer'd nations?
> The soldiers' reverence and the people's love?
> Thy mighty fame and popularity?
> With which thou keepst me still in certain fear,
> Depending on thee for uncertain safety.

(Ellis, 178, v. v. 84–9)

When Phidias and Maximus come running in, Valentinian kills Phidias, but must endure Maximus' scornful reminder that he has killed his 'only stay for sinking greatness'. Valentinian declares Maximus banished but he is unabashed.

> Hold me, ye Gods, and judge our passions rightly,
> Lest I should kill him, kill this luxurious worm,
> Ere yet a thought of danger has awak'd him,
> End him even in the midst of night debauches,
> Mounted on a tripos, drinking healths
> With shallow rascals, pimps, buffoons and bawds,
> Who with vile laughter take him in their arms,
> And bear the drunken Caesar to his bed,
> Where to the scandal of all majesty,
> At every gasp he belches provinces,
> Kisses off fame, and at the Empire's ruin,
> Enjoys his costly whore.

(Ellis, 180, v. v. 138–49)

Valentinian demands to know why Maximus is prepared to kill him, and he answers bluntly:

> Because I have more wit than honesty,
> More of thyself, more villainy than virtue,
> More passion, more revenge and more ambition
> Than foolish honour and fantastic glory.

(Ellis, 181, v. v. 196–9)

Valentinian repents the murder of his true defender as if he had met his 'father in the dark, and striving for the way had murder'd him', but Maximus is unmoved. Valentinian brings death upon himself by one last terrible taunt:

> Would the Gods raise Lucina from the grave,
> And fetter thee but while I might enjoy her,
> Before thy face I'd ravish her again.

(Ellis, 183, v. v. 248–50)

As he hears the soldiers coming Valentinian is confident that they will kill the traitor Maximus, but when they enter they kill him instead.

Valentinian is far more subversive than Rochester's original play *Sodom*, written immediately afterward. Scholars are squeamish about fathering *Sodom* on Rochester, but it does him less discredit than other works that are willingly attributed to him. In many ways *Sodom* is a parody of *Valentinian*; the maids of honour, for example, defend their submission to the king's peculiar sexual demands as the subjects' duty of passive obedience. King Bolloxinian rules the country with his penis because his interest is being loved rather than feared, and the servile nation complies. His barren wife Cuntigratia is as recognizable as Catherine of Braganza as Bolloxinian is as Charles. By excluding all referents to anything beyond the cloaca, *Sodom* becomes a lampoon of lampoons. Court satires like 'Signor Dildo' accuse court ladies of recourse to dildoes of all shapes and sizes; in *Sodom* Lady Officina, the Groom of the Stole, administers pleasure with a dildo to the queen while the Maids of Honour apply dildoes to themselves, in a mockery of court protocol. The inevitable ensues and the entire realm collapses in chaos.

> The young who ne'er on Nature did impose
> To rob her charter or pervert her laws
> Are taught at last to break all former vows
> And do what Love and Nature disallows.[6]

(ll. 32–5)

Bolloxinian asserts his divine right.

> Why did the gods that gave me leave to be
> A king not grant me immortality,
> To be a substitute for heaven at will?
> I scorn the gift. I'll reign and bugger still.

(ll. 54–7)

Fire engulfs Sodom and the curtain falls.

Sodom is an exercise in the same genre as Jarry's *Le Roi Ubu* or *Derek and Clive* by Peter Cook and Dudley Moore, in which the grotesque obscene becomes a style like any other. Outrage interacts with disgust to produce a kind of amazed melancholy, a mood which we can find in Rochester at his most despairing.

Sodom is like other works of Rochester's in that it could have been written by an uproarious committee of wits whose imaginations became more outrageous as the levels in their flagons went down. It is even possible to imagine the paper circulating in a kind of game in which each of the company had to add a speech or couplet capping the last. As *Sodom* needs a chorus who can strum harps with their penises or sound jews' harps through their vaginas, we may assume that it was never performed.

The same is probably true of the piece of street theatre in which Rochester set up a mountebank's stall in Tower Street and attracted a large clientele of all classes of people. There was a precedent for this kind of performance art. In 1663 Pepys described Sir Charles Sedley as

> coming in open day into the Balcone and showed his nakedness – acting all the postures of lust and buggery that could be imagined, and abusing of scripture and, as it were, from thence preaching a Mountebanke sermon from that Pulpitt, saying that there he hath to sell such a Pouder as should make all the cunts in town run after him – a thousand people standing underneath to see and hear him.
>
> And that being done, he took a glass of wine and washed his prick in it and then drank it off; and then took another and drank the King's health.[7]

For this 'riot' Chief-Justice Foster of the King's Bench fined Sedley the swingeing sum of £500. Buckhurst was apparently arraigned along with Sedley, but his role in the affair is unclear.

The evidence for Rochester's performance as a mountebank is of two kinds. The first kind consists in a series of printed texts. In both the British Library and the library of Trinity College, Cambridge, can be found a copy of an undated, anonymously printed quarto pamphlet headed 'To all Gentlemen, Ladies, and others, whether of City, Town or Country: Alexander Bendo wisheth all Health and Prosperity'.[8] In 1691 Tonson printed a fairly accurate transcription of this text, a circumstance which should be enough to cast doubt on Wing's conjectural date of printing, which is given as 1700. The text printed by Curll in 1709 is derived from the same text but includes some interpolated material. The second kind of evidence is the legend as embellished by posthumous commentators. Burnet tells us that Rochester, having disgraced himself with the King, 'disguised himself so that his dearest friends would not have known him and set up in Tower Street for an Italian Mountebank where he had a Stage and practised Physick for some weeks'.[9] In 1687 Thomas Allcock prepared a New Year's gift for the poet's eldest daughter consisting of a transcription of Rochester's bill with a long and rather fanciful introduction, describing how the poet disguised himself with a fake beard, an antique cap, an old green gown lined with vari-coloured fur, and a yellow metal chain and medallion encrusted with fake jewels. According to Allcock, for weeks the poet conducted a roaring trade, taking on numbers of workers who prepared fake medicines from disgusting ingredients in a laboratory that clients could visit to watch them at it.[10]

A seventeenth-century mountebank's bill is a typical handbill, that is, a single sheet of paper, closely printed because ink was cheaper than paper. Alexander Bendo's eight-page pamphlet is, being printed expansively in a large fount with elegant margins, prodigal in its use of paper. It makes a display of the 'doctor's' name in capitals at the top of the first page and the bottom of the last, when most such bills mention no name at all, but only the 'high-German doctor' or some such. The name itself is a clue, the initials 'A. B.' standing for 'Any Body', being a common way of indicating an author who wishes to remain anonymous. The usual mountebank bill is addressed to no one, merely giving in impersonal terms the news that a great practitioner has arrived in town, and setting forth the extraordinary qualities, practices and products that he has at his disposal. Rochester addresses an elite public. The last thing that genuine mountebanks disquisit upon is charlatanry; Rochester's pamphlet, here quoted in its original form, is about nothing else:

> this city (as most great ones are) has ever been infested with a numerous company of such whose arrogant Confidence, backing their ignorance, has enabled them to impose upon the people, either premeditated cheats, or at best the palpable, dull and empty mistakes of their self-deluded imaginations, in Physick, Chymical and Galenick, in Astrology, Physiognomy, Palmistry, Mathematics, Alchimy, and even Government it self: . . .[11]

A mountebank who persists in reminding people that they are being practised on by a 'Bastard Race of Quacks and Cheats' will hardly do well. Rochester turns the irony repeatedly upon itself:

if I appear to anyone like a Counterfeit, even for the sake of that chiefly ought I to be construed as a true man, who is the Counterfeit's example, his original, and that which he employs his pains and industry and pains to imitate and copy? Is it therefore my fault if the Cheat by his Wits and Endeavours makes himself so like me, that consequently I cannot avoid resembling of him; Consider pray the Valiant and the Coward, the wealthy Merchant and the Bankrupt, the Politician and the Fool, they are the same in many things and differ in but one alone. The Valiant man holds up his head, looks confidently about him, wears a Sword, courts a Lord's Wife and owns it; so does the Coward, one only point of Honour, and that's Courage, (which like false metal one onlyy trial can discover) makes the distinction.

The Bankrupt walks the Exchange, buys, bargains, draws Bills and accepts them with the richest, whilst Paper and Credit are current coin; that which makes the difference is real Cash, a great defect indeed, and yet but one, and that the last found out...

What we have here is a satirical address the like of which we shall not see again until Swift begins to practise what Vieth calls the straight-faced mode. Rochester is setting forth charlatanry as a prerequisite for any kind of success in a system based on fraud.

It is possible that people who picked up Rochester's bill sought him out at the address given and Rochester may have found that he had to produce some sort of stock in trade if he was to escape their ire, but such a situation cannot have lasted for weeks. The wealthy and powerful Society of Apothecaries was jealous of its privilege; if there is no mention of Rochester's spectacular performance in Tower Street in the transactions of the society Allcock's tale can hardly be true. The bill is real enough, but the weeks-long masquerade, which Hamilton further embellishes in the *Memoirs of the Comte de Gramont*, is legend.

7

Doubt's Boundless Sea

Burnet tells us that, when 18-year-old Rochester was aboard the *Revenge* off the coast of Norway, he and two other 'King's Letter men', Edward Montague and John Windham, discussed their likely fate:

> The Earl of Rochester, and the last of these, entered into a formal Engagement, not without Ceremonies of Religion, that if either of them died, he should appear, and give the other notice of the future State, if there was any.[1]

The pact was absurd, but the contradiction that made it so is fundamental to Rochester's thinking; his faith was as instinctive as his scepticism was rational. He could no more give up the one than he could escape from the other. (Soon afterwards, as Montague stood supporting Windham whose knees had given way with terror, a single shot passed through Windham, killing him outright, and tore away Montague's belly, so that he died within the hour.)

Anne Rochester had bred her son on the Protestant Bible; biblical ideas and tenets had formed the very fabric of his personality. His poems and letters are full of echoes of the biblical readings and prayers of his youth, often turned upside down or used ironically.[2] Like the devil, Rochester could cite scripture to his purpose, and, like the devil, he was a believer. Rochester's belief was not of the complacent kind that sees its justification in everyday phenomena. All about him but above all at court he saw God being mocked, and by none more impudently than the clerics who accumulated wealth and power through the church of which the dissolute and faithless King was the head. In retreat from conventional hypocrisies Rochester found himself driven into a byroad of English thought, that finds more merit in faith because it is irrational. Those who believe that doubt is a necessary concomitant of the use of rational intelligence and that the only salvation from the torment of doubt is to accept the role of God's fool have been called Christian Pyrrhonists, after the sceptic Greek philosopher Pyrrho. The Christian Pyrrhonist acknowledges his scepticism within the framework of faith and his struggle towards God as a dangerous journey within his own mind. Christian Pyrrhonism inspires Montaigne's 'Apology for Raymond Sebondé', Erasmus' *Encomium morae*, and Hamlet's agonized reflections:

> Sure he that made us with such large discourse,
> Looking before and after, gave us not
> That capability and god-like reason
> To fust in us unus'd.

> (*Hamlet*, IV. iv. 36–9)

Rochester is the intellectual heir of Donne, who in his fourth satire upheld doubt as a moral duty.

> doubt wisely, in strange way
> To stand enquiring right, is not to stray;
> To sleep, or run wrong is: on a huge hill
> Cragg'd, and steep, Truth stands, and he that will
> Reach her, about must, and about must go...

In Charles's court, where a thick crust of religious accoutrement and ceremonial protected a soft core of cynical indifference, Rochester's faith had taken a hammering. He had been prepared to love his King as he loved God, and his disillusionment with his King affected his trust in God. Yet even when Rochester appears to preach nihilism the result is a thoroughly Christian paradox as in his best-known poem *Upon Nothing*. Disbelief underlies all Rochester's satire, whether it deals with 'the perfect joy of being well-deceived' in love and loyalty or the expectation of some future good that dupes the oppressed into putting up with present evil. To write upon nothing as the only thing that was real was the inevitable expression of Rochester's deep distrust of the society whose workings he had been able to see with revolting clarity in the forcing house of the court.

> Though mysteries are barred from laic eyes
> And the divine alone with warrant pries
> Into thy bosom, where thy truth in private lies,

Yet this of thee the wise may truly say,
Thou from the virtuous nothing dost delay,
And to be part of thee the wicked wisely pray.

Great Negative, how vainly would the wise
Enquire, define, distinguish, teach, devise,
Didst Thou not stand to point their blind philosophies!

(Walker, 63, ll. 22–30)

If Rochester had been a true libertine he would have lived as his peace-loving King did, untroubled by the strugglings of conscience and ready to ignore any principle that might prove inconvenient. The King avoided conflict as assiduously as Rochester sought it. Hardly a month went by in which Rochester was not implicated in some fracas. Some would say that this was simply because he was quarrelsome when drunk, which prompts a further question: why was he so often drunk? A tension between the necessity of doubting and the longing for belief tugs at even his most lyrical writing.

Editorially *Upon Nothing* presents a typical Rochesterian conundrum; because others of his contemporaries were exercising their wit on the trope that everything that is came from nothing and may be nothing after all, what have been interpreted as echoes of Rochester may be contemporary expressions of a contemporary talking point. Cowley had slightly laboured the idea of creation out of nothing in the *Davideis*, unconcerned that his revelling in contradiction might be revealing a nonsensicality in the idea. The *Davideis*, a mildly ludicrous celebration of Charles II as the biblical King David, begged for a Rochester or a Rochester/Buckingham or a Rochester/Buckingham/Fleetwood Shepherd to tease out some of the implications of the view that kingship like everything else came out of the void. *Upon Nothing* survives in rather more than the twenty-one contemporary manuscripts listed by Walker (173–4), and was printed twice in broadside in 1679. It is a startlingly clever exploration of a paradox but, even without the problems of attribution, it would not of itself entitle Rochester to the stature of tragic satirist.

In the winter of 1674–5 Rochester made a much more serious attempt to confront his own disillusion by setting forth the inadequacy of human reason.

> Reason, an *ignis fatuus* in the mind,
> Leaving the light of nature, sense, behind,
> Pathless and dangerous wandering ways it takes,
> Through error's fenny bogs and thorny brakes,
> Whilst the misguided follower climbs with pain
> Mountains of whimseys, heaped in his own brain;
> Stumbling from thought to thought, falls headlong down
> Into doubt's boundless sea...
>
> (Walker, 92, ll. 12–19)

A Satire against Mankind has a distinguished literary pedigree, being descended from Juvenal's fifteenth satire via Boileau's eighth. It is a real *satura* or mixed dish, for passages of sustained tragic intensity alternate with droll or distracted asides. The hectic life journey of the rational animal winds down to utter bleakness –

> Then Old Age and Experience, hand in hand,
> Lead him to death and make him understand,
> After a search so painful and so long,
> That all his life he has been in the wrong.
> Huddled in dirt, the reasoning engine lies,
> Who was so proud, so witty, and so wise.
>
> (Walker, 92, ll. 25–30)

Poetry of statement is retrospectively transformed into dramatic monologue by the intrusion of another speaker, 'some formal band and beard' who asks,

> What rage ferments in your degenerate mind
> To make you rail at reason and mankind?
>
> (Walker, 93, ll. 58–9)

and utters a panegyric to the angelic faculty of reason:

> Reason, by whose aspiring influence,
> We take a flight beyond material sense,
> Dive into mysteries, then soaring pierce
> The flaming limits of the universe,
> Search heaven and hell, find out what's acted there,
> And give the world true grounds of hope and fear.
>
> (Walker, 93, ll. 66–71)

The first speaker does not respond, but persists in his tirade, inveighing against religiose romances and academies full of thinking fools. As this gust of exasperation spends itself, he attempts to present his notion of right reason:

> I own right reason which I would obey,
> The reason that distinguishes by sense
> And gives us rules of good and ill from thence,
> That bounds desires with a reforming will,
> To keep 'em more in vigour, not to kill.
>
> (Walker, 94, ll. 99–103)

Rake Rochester has always been assumed to be seeking justification for his own addiction to sensual pleasures, but the invocation of a 'reforming will' that can construct pleasures that do not result in satiety and revulsion should indicate that the justification of self-indulgence is not the point. Human beings are unlike animals in that they are not driven by the instinct for self-preservation, but actively seek their own harm and the harm of others. Human beings, unlike animals, are drawn to sin, guilt and self-destruction. In *A Satire against Mankind* the exercise of human intelligence leads anywhere but to peaceful repose in the knowledge and love of God. Human ingenuity rather develops intricate social structures where morality is obliterated by ruthlessness. Couplet after couplet strikes with a gnomic force that had not been achieved before and would not be achieved again until Dryden hit his stride in *Absalom and Achitophel*.

> Wronged shall he live, insulted o'er, oppressed,
> Who dares be less a villain than the rest.
>
> (Walker, 96, ll. 166–7)

In *A Satire against Mankind* Rochester threw down a gauntlet, not this time to a blade of his own ilk, but to Edward Stillingfleet, whose brilliant career as a religious apologist had reached its apogee with his appointment of chaplain in ordinary to the King:

> 'Hold mighty man!' I cry. 'All this we know,
> From the pathetic pen of Ingelo,
> From Patrick's *Pilgrim*, Stillingfleet's replies,
> And 'tis this very reason I despise,
> This supernatural gift, that makes a mite
> Think he's the image of the Infinite:...
>
> (Walker, 93, ll. 72–7)

As the much-praised author of *A Rational Account of the Grounds of the Protestant Religion*, Stillingfleet hardly expected to be challenged in verse by one of the least significant of the King's drinking companions. It is a matter of some wonder that on 25 February 1675 he took up Rochester's challenge and preached before the King a sermon against the poem, denouncing Rochester as one who defended his own vices by 'trampling underfoot the most noble perfections of his own nature'. At this stage Rochester's satire numbered 174 lines; brooding on Stillingfleet's meteoric career as everybody's favourite theo-logian, loaded with benefices, caressed at court and council board, Rochester took him on in an added 51 lines; he would give way not to a courtier/prelate, but to someone more like the excluded clergymen who found refuge at Adderbury and at his uncle's house in Battersea,

> a meek, humble man of honest sense,
> Who, preaching peace, does practise continence,
> Whose pious life's a proof he does believe
> Mysterious truths which no man can conceive;
> If upon earth there dwell such God-like men,
> I'll here recant my paradox to them...

> (Walker, 97, ll. 216–21)

It is hard to believe that a poet so possessed by moral indignation could have been the most licentious individual at Charles II's licentious court. Rochester's conspicuous failure as a courtier would seem rather to suggest that he was less a villain than the rest and less able to conceal his real loyalties and interests than they. If Stillingfleet had read the poem, his royal parishioner had also read it and realized that Rochester could no longer stomach court life. It was at this time that he granted his disappointed and disappointing courtier the Rangership of Woodstock.

This song, first ascribed by Tonson in 1691, might appear to evoke a familiar if rather more than ordinarily complex pyschosexual context:

> Absent from thee I languish still,
> Then ask me not when I return.
> The straying fool, 'twill plainly kill,
> To wish all day, all night to mourn.

Dear, from thine arms then let me fly,
　　That my fantastic mind may prove
The torments it deserves to try,
　　That tears my fixed heart from my love.

When, wearied with a world of woe,
　　To thy safe bosom I retire,
Where love and peace and truth does flow,
　　May I contented there expire,

Lest once more wandering from that heaven,
　　I fall on some base heart unblest,
Faithless to thee, false, unforgiven,
　　And lose my everlasting rest.

(Walker, 38–9)

This poem has the grammar of a negotiation with a lover, but no ordinary lover's bosom is the source of love *and* peace *and* truth. The human lover whose fantastic mind leads him to seek his own perdition is closely related to the butt of the satire on mankind. The contrast between an earthly lover and a divine one places Rochester's apparently worldly poem in the same spiritual context as the love poems of Quarles or Herbert. Sin and dereliction of the lover's duty are here equated, but the restless movement of the poem enacts the irrepressibility of the relentless fantasy that will not allow the human heart to cleave unto its true love. Divine love stands in the same relation to the speaker as the faithful wife who is its representative on earth but, unlike the neglected wife, divine love does not complain. The poem slyly implies a sophistical expectation that the cuckolded wife be as unchangingly serene as divine love while her human lover behaves as unpredictably as mere humans must do and risk the extreme penalty for rejection of divine love, the loss of eternal rest. In its sophistry, 'Absent from thee' is a typical Cavalier love lyric, but the love that it juggles with is not for woman but for God. At the end of his life Rochester's reckless testing of his physical courage, his sexual hardiesse and the quickness of his wit, all faded into irrelevance as he faced his final ordeal. Long suffering through recurrent and degrading illness led him ultimately to the only unchanging love, the love of God, never to know whether his was 'the perfect joy of being well-deceived' or not. That journey was complete weeks before Burnet fetched up at Rochester's bedside, and is manifest in the poet's divine patience in enduring his visitor's obtuseness.

Abbreviations

BL	British Library
CCC	*Calendar of the Committee for Compounding*
CCSP	*Calender of Clarendon State Papers Preserved in the Bodleian Library*, ed. W. D. Macray and others (Oxford, 1863–1932)
Claydon Papers	Manuscripts of the Verney family preserved at Claydon House, Middle Claydon, Bucks
CSPD	*Calendar of State Papers Domestic*
CTB	*Calendar of Treasury Books*
DNB	*Dictionary of National Biography*
Ellis	*John Wilmot, Earl of Rochester: The Complete Works*, ed. Frank H. Ellis (London and New York, 1994)
Farley-Hills	*Rochester: The Critical Heritage*, ed. D. Farley-Hills (London and New York, 1972; repr. 1995)
HLQ	*Huntington Library Quarterly*
HMC	Historical Manuscripts Commission
LJ	*Lords Journal*
Letters	*The Letters of John Wilmot Earl of Rochester*, ed. Jeremy Treglown (Oxford, 1980)
Pepys	*The Diary of Samuel Pepys*, ed. R. Latham and W. Mathews (London, 1970)
Sandwich MSS	Sandwich family papers preserved at Mapperton, Dorset
V&A	Victoria and Albert Museum

Notes

CHAPTER 1.   INTRODUCTION

1   D. M. Vieth, *Attribution in Restoration Poetry: A Study of Rochester's Poems of 1680* (New Haven and London, 1963), *passim*.

2   'Satire on both Whigs and Tories', Bodleian MS Firth C. 15, fos. 146 ff.

3   *Familiar Letters* (1697), i. 47; *Letters*, 232.

4   Public Record Office, Chancery Lane, C104/110.

5   Various commentators have questioned the reliability of Burnet's account, e.g. Christopher Hill in *Writing and Revolution in Seventeenth Century England* (Brighton, 1985), 310.

6   See e.g. A. B. Worden (ed.), *A Voyce from the Watchtower. Edmund Ludlow*, Part 5 (1660–62).

7   For a detailed discussion of this publication, see *The Collected Works of Katherine Philips, the Matchless Orinda; ii. The Letters*, ed. P. Thomas (Stump Cross, 1990), 196–205. See also G. Greer, 'Honest Sam. Briscoe', in R. Myers and M. Harris (eds.), *A Genius for Letters: Booksellers and Bookselling from the 16th to the 20th Century* (Delaware: Oak Knoll Press, 1995), 33–47.

8   'The Nightingale and the Cuckoo', Northampton Record Office MS Finch-Hatton 258, fo. 8^v.

9   Autograph letter, 22 June [?1671], *Letters*, 67.

10   J. Prinz, *John Wilmot, Earl of Rochester: His Life and Writings* (Leipzig, 1927), 24 n.

11   Samuel Johnson, *The Lives of the Poets*, in Farley-Hills, 204.

12   Anne Wharton, 'Elegie on John Earle of Rochester', ll. 7–9, 30–2, in *The Surviving Works of Anne Wharton*, ed. G. Greer and S. Hastings (Stump Cross, 1997), 140–1.

13   Farley-Hills, 27–9, 36–8.

14   Ibid. 105–6.

CHAPTER 2.   THE POET'S BIOGRAPHY

1   *CSPD 1667*, 339, 450.
2   Claydon Papers, letter of William Denton to Sir Ralph Verney, 6 September 1643.
3   P. R. Newman, *The Old Service: Royalist Regimental Colonels and the Civil War, 1642–46* (Manchester and New York, 1993), 152.
4   *CCSP* iv. 166, 167, 190, 209.
5   *CCC*, 249: 80; Claydon Papers, letter of Lady Sussex to Sir Ralph Verney, 6 May 1645.
6   *The Life and Times of Anthony à Wood*, ed. Andrew Clark (Oxford, 1892), ii. 492.
7   *CCSP* i. 395.
8   *CCSP* ii. 155–64.
9   *CCSP* ii. 302, 304, 317; iii. 337, 351, 357, 381.
10 Treglown is mistaken in identifying the son about whom Clarendon wrote to Wilmot in August 1653 as the poet; this son, perhaps from Wilmot's first marriage, died of a malignant fever in October the same year.
11 Claydon Papers, letter of John Cary to Sir Ralph Verney, 23 February 1660.
12 *Athenae oxoniensis*, ed. P. Bliss (3rd edn., 1813–20), 1232.
13 *CSPD 1660–1*, 523; also *CTB 1660–7*, 244, 253, 372, 699.
14 V. de Sola Pinto, *Enthusiast in Wit: A Portrait of John Wilmot, Earl of Rochester, 1647–1680* (London, 1962).
15 Claydon Papers, letter of John Cary to Sir Ralph Verney, 14 April 1679.
16 Claydon Papers, letters of John Cary to Sir Ralph Verney, 30 December 1685 and 14 February 1687.
17 Letter from Charles II to Henrietta, Duchess of Orleans, 26 January 1664; C. H. Hartmann, *Charles II and Madame* (London, 1934), 135–6.
18 Sandwich MSS, Letters from Ministers, i, fo. 39; letter of Lord Arlington to Lord Sandwich, 5 December 1664; see also *Savile Correspondence*, ed. W. D. Cooper (London, 1858), 5.
19 BL MS Loan 57, letter 4 of Sir Allen Apsley to Lady Apsley, 30 May 1665. Twenty years later the Countess was successfully to 'surprise' her son's youngest daughter, Lady Malet Wilmot, in the garden of her maternal grandmother's house, whisk her into her coach and carry her off to Adderbury. On that occasion the Countess was charged with kidnapping and faced trial at the Aylesbury Assizes, but, by appearing in the courtroom in her full grandeur attended by the even more magnificant figure of another granddaughter, the Countess of Abingdon, she succeeded in beating the rap and

keeping the child (BL Add. MS 38,012, fo. 27, letter from Charles Bertie to Mr Moore, 23 June 1685).

20 *CSPD 1664–1665*, 389.
21 *CSPD 1664–1665*, 435.
22 *Letters*, 46–9.
23 *CSPD 1665–1666*, 35.
24 Ibid. 310.
25 BL MS Carte 75, fo. 477, and 74, fo. 343; see also Pepys, 20 August 1666, vii. 260 and n.
26 Pepys, 25 November 1666, vii. 385 and n.
27 Claydon Papers, letter from Margaret Elmes to Sir Ralph Verney, 31 January 1666/7.
28 Claydon Papers, letter of Lady Rochester to Sir Ralph Verney, 15 February 1666/7.
29 It seems that the bulk of the inheritance was settled on the heirs of Elizabeth's body; though Rochester was engulfed in debt at the time of his death, his three daughters were wealthy and made good matches. See e.g. Claydon Papers, letter of Lady Rochester to Sir Ralph Verney, 14 April 1679.
30 Claydon Papers, letter of John Cary to Sir Ralph Verney, 13 April 1667.
31 *CSPD 1666–1667*, 560; *Letters*, 16, 51–2.
32 *CSPD 1667*, 582; *Letters*, 16.
33 For a succinct account of the background to these events, see Bruce Yardley, 'George Villiers, Duke of Buckingham and the Politics of Toleration', *HLQ* 55 (Spring, 1992), 320–1, and Clayton Roberts, 'The Impeachment of the Earl of Clarendon', *Cambridge History Journal*, 13 (1957), 1–18.
34 Pepys, 2 December 1668, ix. 382.
35 According to the Earl of Sandwich (Sandwich MSS, Journals, ix. 116–18).
36 Pepys, 17 February 1669, ix. 451–2.
37 Claydon Papers, letters from Margaret Elmes to Sir Ralph Verney, 17, 18, March 1668/9; see also BL Add. MS 36916, fo. 127.
38 Ibid., letter from Margaret Elmes to Sir Ralph Verney, 25 March 1668/9.
39 Ibid., Letter from John Cary to Sir Ralph Verney, 29 April 1669.
40 Ibid., Letter from John Cary to Sir Ralph Verney, 6 May 1669.
41 *Letters*, 55; HMC 7th report, app. 531a, 488b.
42 *LJ*.
43 Claydon Papers, letter of John Cary to Sir Ralph Verney, 30 March 1670.
44 Ibid., letter of John Cary to Sir Ralph Verney, 26 April 1670.
45 Rochester's holograph, BL MS Harl. 7003, fo. 202; *Letters*, 58.

46 Claydon Papers, letter of John Cary to Sir Ralph Verney, 22 July 1670.

47 Ibid., letter of John Cary to Sir Ralph Verney, 30 November 1670.

48 Ibid., letter of Anne Rochester to Sir Ralph Verney, 14 April 1679. Anne Rochester continued to finance Adderbury until the Lee girls' trusts were wound up in 1979. After Elizabeth Wilmot's sudden death she was able to remain in possession of Adderbury as the guardian of the poet's three daughters. At the time of her death in 1696 she was living in London.

49 Rochester's holograph, BL MS Harl. 7003, fo. 235, franked Av. 6; *Letters*, 64.

50 *CTB* 1672.

51 Rochester's holograph, BL MS Harl. 7003, fo. 201; *Letters*, 65.

52 Claydon Papers, letter from Sir Ralph Verney to Edmund Verney, 14 December 1671.

53 Ibid., letter from Sir Ralph Verney to Edmund Verney, 28 December 1671. Richard Newport is mentioned by Pepys as one of the Ballers 'whose mad bawdy talk made [his] heart ache' (31 May 1688), Pepys, ix. 218.

54 Belvoir Castle, Rutland MSS, xviii, item 210, letter from Lady Mary Bertie to Katherine Noel, ? July 1672.

55 *Letters*, 83–4.

56 Rochester's holograph, BL MS Harl. 7003, fo. 191; *Letters*, 242 and n. Treglown gives this letter a putative date of 1680, the year of the poet's death. If the letter's argument, that the soul of a man who 'counts anything a benefit [that is] obtained with flattery, fear and service' would be better placed in a dog's body does not have the poet repeating himself, he has not yet written *A Satire against Mankind*, which can be dated to the last weeks of 1674.

57 The grants of the various offices connected with Woodstock were vaguely expressed and caused great confusion; Rochester was obliged several times to enter caveats to protect his right which extended only to the lodge and the adjacent walk (*CSPD 1675–1676*, 320, 341, 367, 473).

58 Letter from William Harbord to the Earl of Essex, 22 December 1674, quoted in *Poems and Letters of Andrew Marvell*, ed. H. M. Margoliouth (Oxford, 1927), ii. 336.

59 A newsletter alleges that Rochester shouted 'Dost thou stand there to fuck time?'

60 Claydon Papers, letter of John Verney to Edmund Verney, 29 June 1676.

61 BL Add. MS. 18, 730, fos. 15, 15^v; Claydon Papers, letter of John Cary to Sir Ralph Verney, 27 September 1676.

62 *CSPD 1676–1677*; *Letters*, 143–4.

63 *HMC 29, Portland*, iii. 355.

64 Letter from Andrew Marvell to Sir Edward Harley, *Poems and Letters of Andrew Marvell*, ii. 355.
65 *Letters*, 144.
66 Claydon Papers, letters from Lady Penelope Osborne to Sir Ralph Verney, 2 and 16 October 1677.
67 See *The Surviving Works of Anne Wharton*, ed. G. Greer and S. Hastings (Stump Cross, 1997), 99–100.
68 Claydon Papers, draft letter of Edmund Verney to Sir Ralph Verney, 23 September 1678; see also letter of Dr Denton to Sir Ralph Verney, 12 September 1678.
69 Robert Wolseley, Preface to *Valentinian* (London, 1685).
70 Claydon Papers, letter from John Cary to Sir Ralph Verney, 3 February 1679.
71 Claydon Papers, letters from John Cary to Sir Ralph Verney, 1 June 1680, and from Sir Ralph Verney to John Verney, 7 June 1680.
72 There is no truth in Prinz's bizarre assertion that the milk of asses injected with mercury was a preferred way of treating venereal disease. All kinds of respectable people, including the upright Sir Ralph Verney, drank ass's milk to build themselves up after wasting fevers.
73 J. Prinz, *John Wilmot, Earl of Rochester, His Life and Writings* (Leipzig, 1927), 300.

CHAPTER 3. THE POET AT COURT

1 E. E. Duncan Jones, 'Dryden, Benserade and Marvell', *HLQ* 54 (Winter, 1991), 74.
2 Buckingham's holograph, BL MS Harl. 7003, fo. 276; *Letters*, 51.
3 Rochester's holograph, Walker, 40–1 and 249; see also D. M. Vieth, in *Papers of the Bibliographical Society of America*, 54 (1960), 147–62, and 55 (1961), 130–3.
4 Walker chooses to publish the 23-stanza version as he found it in V&A MS Dyce 43. Harold Love doubts that it is by Rochester; see 'A Restoration Lampoon in Transmission and Revision: Rochester's (?) "Signior Dildoe" ', *Studies in Bibliography*, 46 (1993), 250–62, and 'A New "A" text of "Signior Dildo" ', *Studies in Bibliography*, 49 (1996), 169–75.
5 *Poems and Letters of Andrew Marvell*, ed. H. M. Margoliouth (Oxford, 1927), i. 307.

CHAPTER 4. THE POET OF LOVE

1 *A Collection of Poems, Written upon Several Occasions, by Several Persons* (1672), 53–4 (second pagination).
2 J. H. Wilson, *Court Satires of the Restoration* (Columbus, OH, 1979), 169–0 and *passim*.
3 Farley-Hills, 28.
4 The text from *A Collection of Poems, Written upon Several Occasions, by Several Persons* (1672), 259, conflated with Tonson (1691), 21.
5 Roma Gill notes in her introduction to the first volume of *The Complete Works of Christopher Marlowe* (Oxford, 1987), 'unmistakeable confusions of "my" and "thy"...the explanation is to be found in Marlowe's signature, where the M is very like the character for "th" in Elizabethan secretary hand' (p. 11).
6 Buckingham's holograph, printed in *Buckingham: Public and Private Man: The Prose, Poems and Commonplace Book of George Villiers, Second Duke of Buckingham (1628–1687)* ed. Christine Phipps (New York and London, 1985), 170–1.

CHAPTER 5. THE FEMALE IMPERSONATOR

1 Gilbert Burnet, in Farley-Hills, 64.
2 'To my Lord Ignorant', in Ben Jonson, *The Complete Poems*, ed. George Parfitt (London, 1988), 37.
3 'Cloe to Artimesa', in *Eighteenth Century Women Poets: An Oxford Anthology,* ed. Roger Lonsdale (Oxford, 1989), 83.
4 *A New Miscellany* (1720), 124–5.
5 See the account of Wolseley in *The Surviving Works of Anne Wharton*, ed. G. Greer and S. Hastings (Stump Cross, 1997), 87–90.
6 *Letters*, 115–16.

CHAPTER 6. THE POET IN THE THEATRE

1 Farley-Hills, 31.
2 Ellis reprints the corrupt text from *Poems on Affairs of State* (1697), where this couplet appears after line 13; Vieth and Walker both prefer the reading that places it at the end of the poem.
3 Farley-Hills, 186.
4 *The Works of Aphra Behn*, ed. J. Todd (London, 1992), i. 160.
5 A. C. Sprague, *Beaumont and Fletcher on the Restoration Stage* (facs. repr. New York, 1965), 59.

6 *Sodom* is not printed or even mentioned by Professor Ellis. These quotations are taken from Paddy Lyons's edition, with punctuation corrected by the author.
7 Pepys, iv, 209, 1 July 1663.
8 BL, shelf-mark C. 112, fo. 9 (41). All quotations are drawn from this exemplum.
9 Farley-Hills, 54.
10 University of Nottingham MS 1489; see also Hamilton, *Mémoires du Comte de Gramont* (1931), 258.
11 BL. Ellis, who seems to be unaware that copies of the original printing have survived, uses Curll on the mistaken assumption that, being longer, it is 'perfect'.

CHAPTER 7. DOUBT'S BOUNDLESS SEA

1 Farley-Hills, 52.
2 Larry Carver, 'Rascal before the Lord; Rochester's Religious Rhetoric', D. M. Vieth (ed.), *John Wilmot, Earl of Rochester: Critical Essays* (London, 1988); J. Treglown, 'The Satirical Inversion of some English courses in Rochester's Poetry', *Review of English Studies*, NS, 24 (1973), 46–7.

Select Bibliography

EDITIONS

Ellis, Frank H. (ed.), *John Wilmot, Earl of Rochester. The Complete Works* (Harmondsworth and New York, 1994), accepts ninety poems as authentic Rochester, rejecting one attribution accepted by both Vieth and Walker, and five of Walker's six additions to the Vieth canon, and introducing nine new attributions of his own. This edition has the merit of including all Rochester's dramaturgy (except *Sodom*, which is nowhere mentioned). Ellis also prints a version of Rochester's mountebank pamphlet, based on Curll (1709), apparently because he was unaware of the survival of two exempla of the earlier printing.

Lyons, Paddy (ed.), *Rochester: Complete Poems and Plays* (London and Rutland, VT, 1993), may take credit for being the only editor to print *Sodom*, although in a corrupt version. As well as the plays and the mountebank pamphlet Lyons prints 103 poems as being genuine Rochester, including all but one of eighty-four poems printed by Vieth, rejecting all but three of Walker's additions to the canon, and all but one of Ellis's, and adding fourteen new attributions of his own, none of which does Rochester much credit.

Vieth, David M. (ed.), *The Complete Poems of John Wilmot, Earl of Rochester* (New Haven and London, 1968), seeks to establish a canon of seventy-six poems arranged under four headings as 'Prentice Work 1665–1671', 'Early Maturity 1672–1673', 'Tragic Maturity 1674–1675' and 'Disillusionment and Death 1676–1680'. Such a chronological framework, necessitating an attempt to print the poems in order of composition, involves the editor in considerable speculation. Both orthography and punctuation are modernized without regard for occasional violence to syntax and patterning. Vieth also prints eight 'Poems possibly by Rochester', which include the three poems published while the poet was at Oxford and the song from *Valentinian*, which are accepted by other editors as by Rochester.

Walker, Keith (ed.), *The Poems of John Wilmot, Earl of Rochester* (Oxford and New York, 1984), printed all but one of Vieth's eighty-four poems and adds ten others, on fairly convincing grounds. Walker provides valuable textual apparatus that collates almost all the contemporary manuscript copies and printings of Rochester's poems, making this far and away the most useful edition of the poems, though its readability is not helped by his scrupulousness in reproducing the spelling and punctuation of his copy-texts.

Treglown, Jeremy (ed.), *The Letters of John Wilmot, Earl of Rochester* (Oxford, 1980). Treglown's introduction is the most useful biography of Rochester to date. Some caution must be used when dealing with the letters; dates, recipients and addresses may be silent conjecture.

BIBLIOGRAPHY

Prinz, Johannes, *John Wilmot, Earl of Rochester: His Life and Writings* (Leipzig, 1927).

CRITICAL AND LITERARY-HISTORICAL STUDIES

Carver, Larry, 'Rochester's Valentinian', *Restoration and Eighteenth Century Theatre Review*, 4/1 (Summer, 1989), 25–38.

Erskine-Hill, Howard, 'Rochester: Augustan or Explorer?', in G. R. Hibbard (ed.), *Renaissance and Modern Essays Presented to Vivian de Sola Pinto in Celebration of his Seventieth Birthday*, (London and New York, 1966), 51–64.

Farley-Hills, David, *Rochester's Poetry* (Totowa, NJ, 1978).

—— (ed.) *Rochester: The Critical Heritage* (London and New York, 1972; repr. 1995).

Fujimura, T. H., 'Rochester's "Satyr against Mankind": An Analysis', *Studies in Philology*, 60 (1958), 576–90.

Griffin, Dustin H., *Satires against Man: The Poems of Rochester* (Berkeley and Los Angeles, and London, 1973).

Love, Harold, 'Scribal Texts and Literary Communities: The Rochester Circle and Osborn b. 105', *Studies in Bibliography*, 42 (1989), 212–35.

Main, C. F., 'The Right Vein of Rochester's *Satyr*', in Rudolf Kirk and C. F. Main (eds.), *Essays in Literary History Presented to J. Milton French* (New Brunswick, NJ, 1960).

Miller, H. K., 'The Paradoxical Encomium with Special Reference to its Vogue in England, 1600–1800', *Modern Philology*, 53 (1956), 145–79.

Pinto, Vivian de Sola, *Enthusiast in Wit: A Portrait of John Wilmot, Earl of Rochester 1647–1680* (London, 1962).

—— 'Rochester and Dryden', *Renaissance and Modern Studies*, 5 (1961), 29–48.

—— 'John Wilmot, Earl of Rochester and the Right Veine of Satire', in William R. Keast (ed)., *Seventeenth-Century English Poetry: Modern Essays in Criticism* (New York, 1962), 350–74.

Righter, Anne (later Barton), 'John Wilmot, Earl of Rochester', Chatterton Lecture, *Proceedings of the British Academy*, 53 (1968), 47–69.

Thormählen, Marianne, *Rochester: The Poems in Context* (Cambridge, 1993).

Treglown, Jeremy (ed.) *Spirit of Wit: Reconsiderations of Rochester* (Hamden, CT, 1982).

—— 'The Satirical Inversion of some English Sources in Rochester's Poetry', *Review of English Studies*, NS 24 (1973), 42–8.

—— 'Rochester and Davenant', *Notes and Queries*, 221 (December 1976), 554–9.

Vieth, David M., *Attribution in Restoration Poetry: A Study of Rochester's 'Poems' of 1680* (New Haven and London, 1968).

—— (ed.), *John Wilmot, Earl of Rochester: Critical Essays* (New York, 1988).

—— 'Two Rochester Songs', *Notes and Queries*, 201 (August 1956), 338–9.

—— and Griffin Dustin, *Rochester and Court Poetry* (London, 1988).

Whitfield, Francis, *Beast in View: A Study of the Earl of Rochester's Poetry* (London and Cambridge, MA, 1936).

Williamson, George, *The Proper Wit of Poetry* (Chicago, 1961).

GENERAL

Addy, John, *Sin and Society in the Seventeenth Century* (London, 1989).

Allen Don Cameron, *Doubt's Boundless Sea: Skepticism and Faith in the Renaissance* (Baltimore, 1964).

Behrens, B., 'The Whig Theory of the Constitution in the Reign of Charles II', *Cambridge Historical Journal*, 7/1 (1941).

Chernaik, Warren, *The Poetry of Limitation: A Study of Edmund Waller* (New Haven, 1968).

Colie, Rosemary, *Paradoxica epidemica: The Renaissance Tradition of Paradox*, (Princeton, NJ, 1966).

Doody, Margaret Anne, *The Daring Muse: Augustan Poetry Reconsidered* (Cambridge, 1985).

Elkin, P. K., *The Augustan Defence of Satire* (Oxford, 1973).

Farley-Hills, David, *The Benevolence of Laughter: Comic Poetry of the Commonwealth and Restoration* (London and Basingstoke, 1974).

Fletcher, Anthony, and Roberts, Peter (eds.), *Religion, Culture and Society in Early Modern Britain* (Cambridge, 1994).

―――― and Stevenson, John (eds.), *Order and Disorder in Early Modern England* (Cambridge, 1985).

Goldie, Mark, Tim Harris and Paul Seaward (eds.), *The Politics of Religion in Restoration England* (Oxford, 1990).

Harley, David, 'Political Post-Mortems and Morbid Anatomy in Seventeenth Century England', *Social History of Medicine*, 7 (1994), 1–28.

Harris, Tim, *London Crowds in the Reign of Charles II: Propaganda and Politics from the Restoration to the Exclusion Crisis* (Cambridge, 1987).

Hill, Christopher, *The Century of Revolution 1603–1714* (Wokingham, 1980).

Hoopes, R., *Right Reason in the English Renaissance* (Cambridge, MA, 1962).

Hutton, Ronald, *The Restoration: A Political and Religious History of England and Wales 1658–1687* (Oxford, 1985)

Jack, Ian, *Augustan Satire: Intention and Idiom in English Poetry 1660–1750* (Oxford, 1952).

Jones, George Hilton, *Convergent Forces: Immediate Causes of the Revolution of 1688 in England* (Ames, IA, 1990).

Jones, J. R., *Country and Court: England 1658–1714* (London, 1978).

Lord, George deF. *et al.* (eds.), *Poems on Affairs of State: Augustan Satirical Verse 1660–1714* (New Haven, 1963–75).

Love, Harold, *Scribal Publication in Seventeenth-Century England* (Oxford, 1993).

―――― (ed.), *Restoration Literature: Critical Approaches* (Oxford, 1972).

McKeon, M., *Politics and Religion in Restoration England* (Cambridge, MA, 1975).

Miller, J., *Restoration England: The Reign of Charles II* (London, 1985).

―――― 'The Potential for Absolutism in later Stuart England', *History*, 69 (1984).

Miner, Earl, *The Restoration Mode from Milton to Dryden* (Princeton, NJ, 1974).

Norbrook, David, *Poetry and Politics in the English Renaissance* (London, 1984).

Ogg, David M., *England in the Reign of Charles II* (Oxford, 1955).

Pooley, Roger, 'Language and Loyalty: Plain Style at the Restoration', *Literature and History*, 6 (1980), 2–18.

Rawson, Claude (ed.), *English Satire and the Satiric Tradition* (Oxford, 1984).

Ricks, Christopher, *English Poetry and Prose 1540–1674* (London, 1970).

Ronalds, F. S., *The Attempted Whig Revolution of 1678–81* (Urbana, IL, 1937).

Scott, Jonathan, *Algernon Sidney and the English Republic, 1623–1677* (Cambridge, 1988).

―――― 'Radicalism and Restoration: The Shape of the Stuart Experience', *Historical Journal*, 31/2 (1988).

―――― *Algernon Sidney and the Restoration Crisis, 1677–1683* (Cambridge, 1991).

Sharpe, K., and   Zwicker, Stephen M., *Politics and Discourse: The Literature and History of Seventeenth-Century England* (Berkeley and Los Angeles, 1987).

Stallybrass, Peter, and White, Allon, *The Politics and Poetics of Transgression* (London, 1986).

Sutherland, James, *English Literature of the Late Seventeenth Century* (Oxford, 1969).

Thompson, Roger, *Unfit for Modest Ears: A Study of Pornographic, Obscene and Bawdy Works Written or Published in England in the Second Half of the Seventeenth Century* (London, 1979).

Smith, H. W., ' "Reason" and the Restoration Ethos', *Scrutiny*, 18 (1951), 118–36.

Webster, C. (ed.), *The Intellectual Revolution of the Seventeenth Century* (London, 1974).

Wilson, John H., *Court Satires of the Restoration* (Columbus, OH, 1978).

―――― *The Court Wits of the Restoration: An Introduction* (Princeton, NJ, 1948).

Winn, James A., *John Dryden and his World* (London, 1987).

Index

Recent and Forthcoming Titles in the New Series of

WRITERS AND THEIR WORK

"...this series promises to outshine its own previously high reputation."
Times Higher Education Supplement

"...will build into a fine multi-volume critical encyclopaedia of English literature."
Library Review & Reference Review

"...Excellent, informative, readable, and recommended."
NATE News

"written by outstanding contemporary critics, whose expertise is flavoured by unashamed enthusiasm for their subjects and the series' diverse aspirations."
Times Educational Supplement

"A useful and timely addition to the ranks of the lit crit and reviews genre. Written in an accessible and authoritative style."
Library Association Record

WRITERS AND THEIR WORK
RECENT & FORTHCOMING TITLES

RECENT & FORTHCOMING TITLES

Title	Author
A Midsummer Night's Dream	Helen Hackett
Vladimir Nabokov	Neil Cornwell
V. S. Naipaul	Suman Gupta
Walter Pater	Laurel Brake
Brian Patten	Linda Cookson
Harold Pinter	Mark Batty
Sylvia Plath	Elisabeth Bronfen
Jean Rhys	Helen Carr
Richard II	Margaret Healy
Dorothy Richardson	Carol Watts
John Wilmot, Earl of Rochester	Germaine Greer
Romeo and Juliet	Sasha Roberts
Christina Rossetti	Kathryn Burlinson
Salman Rushdie	Damian Grant
Paul Scott	Jacqueline Banerjee
The Sensation Novel	Lyn Pykett
P.B. Shelley	Paul Hamilton
Wole Soyinka	Mpalive Msiska
Edmund Spenser	Colin Burrow
J.R.R. Tolkien	Charles Moseley
Leo Tolstoy	John Bayley
Charles Tomlinson	Tim Clark
Anthony Trollope	Andrew Sanders
Victorian Quest Romance	Robert Fraser
Angus Wilson	Peter Conradi
Mary Wollstonecraft	Jane Moore
Women's Gothic	Emma Clery
Virginia Woolf	Laura Marcus
Working Class Fiction	Ian Haywood
W.B. Yeats	Edward Larrissy
Charlotte Yonge	Alethea Hayter

01912 825022

BARTNETT WARD